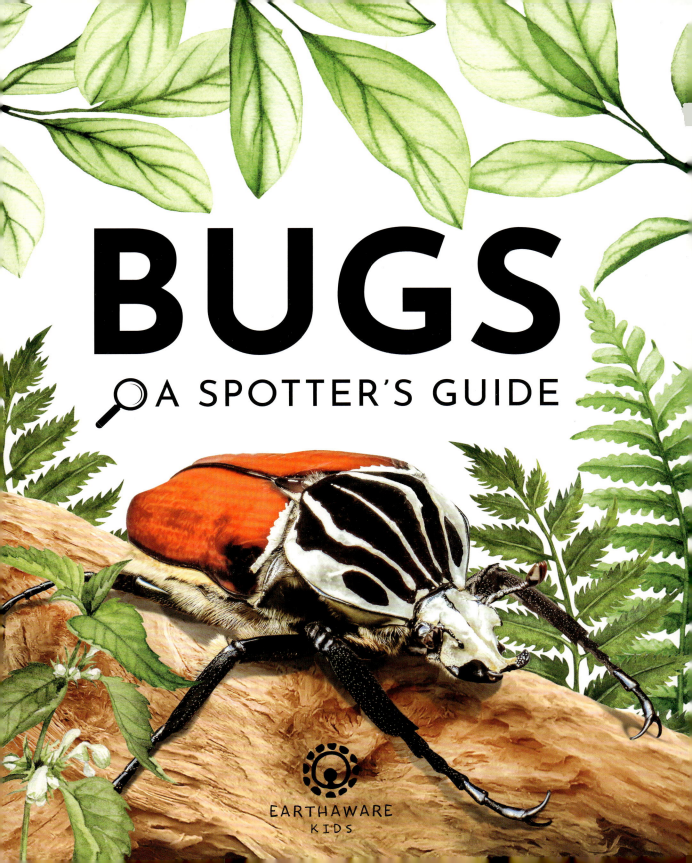

Written by: Pauline Savage
Consultant: Professor Greg Hurst, MA, PhD

Illustrated by: Fiona Osbaldstone

Copyright © EarthAware Kids, 2025

All rights reserved. No part of this publication may be reproduced, distributed, or transmitted in any form or by any means, including photocopying, recording, or other electronic or mechanical methods, without the prior written permission of the publisher, except in the case of brief quotations embodied in critical reviews and certain other noncommercial uses permitted by copyright law.

Published by EarthAware Kids
An imprint of Insight Editions
PO Box 3088
San Rafael, CA 94912
www.insighteditions.com

Weldon Owen Children's Books
Senior Designer: Emma Randall
Editors: Toni Stemp and Eliza Kirby
Managing Editor: Mary Beth Garhart

Insight Editions
Publisher: Raoul Goff
Senior Production Manager: Greg Steffen

ISBN: 979-8-88674-094-3
Manufactured, printed, and assembled in China
First printing, May 2025. DRM0525
10 9 8 7 6 5 4 3 2 1

MIX
Paper | Supporting responsible forestry
FSC® C188448

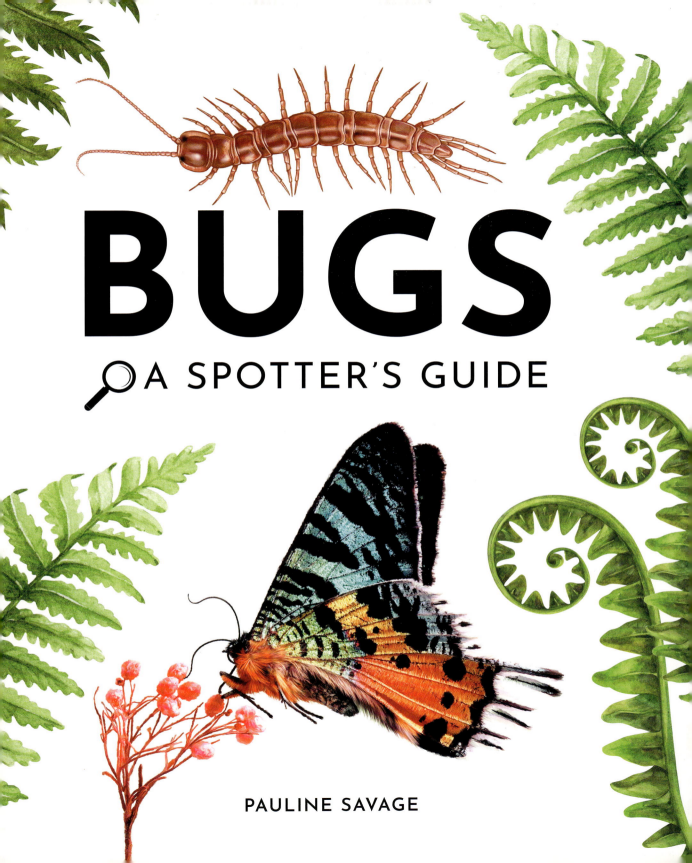

CONTENTS

8   **WELCOME TO THE WORLD OF BUGS**
10   What is a bug?

12   **BUTTERFLIES AND MOTHS**
14   How to spot butterflies and moths
16   American snout, Glasswing
17   Paper kite, Painted lady
18   Red cracker, Tawny coster
19   Orange oakleaf, Postman
20   Monarch
22   Baltimore checkerspot, Cleopatra
23   Apollo, Cairns birdwing
24   Swallowtails
26   Peacock
27   Green hairstreak, Long-tailed skipper
28   Moon moths
30   Hercules moth, Madagascan sunset moth
31   Lobster moth
32   Hawk moths
33   Giant leopard moth, Vampire moth
34   Cinnabar moth, Peppered moth
35   Rosy maple moth, Eight-spotted forester
36   Polyphemus moth
37   Garden tiger moth
38   Regal moth
39   Puss moth

40 ANTS, WASPS, AND BEES
42 How to spot ants, wasps, and bees
44 Leafcutter ant
45 Honeypot ant
46 Siafu ant, Pharaoh ant
47 European wasp, Asian giant hornet
48 Solitary wasps
50 Parasitic wasps
52 Sawfly
53 Oak gall wasp
54 Bees

56 BEETLES
58 How to spot beetles
60 American burying beetle
61 Violin beetle, Rove beetle
62 Large copper dung beetle
63 Giant stag beetle
64 Hercules beetle
66 Whirligig beetle, Fire-colored beetle
67 Great diving beetle, Darkling beetle
68 Jewel beetle, Colorado beetle
69 Flea beetle, Pine chafer
70 Tortoise beetle, Harlequin beetle
71 Long-horned beetle, Bombardier beetle
72 Goliath beetle
73 Aquatic firefly
74 Weevils
76 Orange ladybug
77 Convergent lady beetle
78 Ladybugs

80	**ARACHNIDS**
82	How to spot arachnids
84	Orb weavers
86	Funnel web spider
87	Tarantula, Trapdoor spider
88	Jumping spider
89	Spitting spider, Violin spider
90	Widow spiders
92	House spider, Wolf spider
93	David Bowie huntsman spider
94	Dancing white lady, Brazilian wandering spider
95	Raft spider
96	Mouse spider, Heather spider
97	Flower crab spider
98	Sheep tick
99	Deathstalker scorpion
100	Pseudoscorpion
101	Sun spider, Harvestman
102	Mites
104	**TRUE FLIES**
106	How to spot true flies
108	Stalk-eyed fly
109	Crane fly, Sand fly
110	Drosophila fruit fly, Tephritid fruit fly
111	Black soldier fly

112	Deer fly, Horse fly
113	House fly, Hover fly
114	Mosquitos
116	Green bottle fly, Midge
117	Needle midge
118	Robber fly
119	Hairy bee fly, Tsetse fly

120 TRUE BUGS

122	How to spot true bugs
124	Assassin bug
125	Wheel bug
126	Milkweed bug, Box-elder bug
127	Shield bug, Minstrel bug
128	Water bugs
130	Periodical cicada, Leafhopper
131	Meadow froghopper
132	Oak treehopper
133	Brazilian treehopper
134	Lantern bug
135	Scale insect
136	Black bean aphid
137	Bedbug

138 SMALL ORDERS

140	How to spot small orders
142	Dragonfly
144	Banded demoiselle
145	Eastern dobsonfly
146	Lacewing
147	Antlion
148	Caddisfly
149	Thrip, Mayfly
150	Stonefly
151	Scorpionfly
152	Stick insect
153	Spiny leaf stick insect
154	Earwig, Field grasshopper
155	Locust
156	Jerusalem cricket
157	Field cricket, Great green bush cricket
158	Broad-winged katydid
159	Head louse
160	Human flea
161	Cat flea
162	Mantises
164	American cockroach
165	Termites
166	Woodlouse
167	Silverfish
168	Springtail
169	Centipede, Millipede
170	Caridean shrimp, Tanaid
171	Water flea
172	Ostracod
173	Cyclops copepod

174 INDEX

WELCOME TO THE WORLD OF BUGS

Picture this—you are taking a walk in the countryside. Ants and spiders scuttle at your feet, wasps and bees buzz around flowers, and butterflies and ladybugs are fluttering around, looking for somewhere to lay their eggs.

What else will you see on your imaginary bug-spotting journey?

Monarch butterfly

Funnel web spider

HOW TO USE THIS BOOK 9

Pharoah ant

Woodlouse

BUGS IN DANGER

All over the world, bugs are becoming more scarce. They are threatened by climate change, habitat loss, pollution, and the use of chemicals to protect crops. If a bug becomes extinct, it endangers the animals and plants that rely on it for food and pollination. Bugs do lots of valuable work everywhere—in homes, towns and cities, the countryside—but their survival is at risk.

It's not too late to find a different way to live alongside bugs. You can start right now by reading this book and thinking about what you can do to help.

Seven-spot ladybug

Asian giant hornet

10 HOW TO USE THIS BOOK

WHAT IS A BUG?

There are lots of different types of bugs in this book, from the tiny fairy fly to the giant Goliath beetle. Most of them are insects. These bugs have three body parts—the head, thorax, and abdomen. On the head are two antennae, or feelers. When they become adults, insects have six legs, and most have two pairs of wings.

Leg

Antenna

Head

Thorax

Abdomen

Wings

Crane fly

CHANGING FORM
Most insects go through several changes before they become adults. This is called metamorphosis, and there are four stages.

Egg
Insects begin life as an egg, laid by the adult female.

Life cycle of the peacock butterfly

Larva
A creature called a larva hatches from the egg. Larvae spend their time eating. They molt, or shed skin, several times as they grow.

Adult
The insect emerges from the pupa as an adult. It looks very different from its larval form.

Pupa
The larva builds itself a protective covering called a chrysalis, or cocoon, and becomes a pupa. Inside, it turns to liquid and builds itself a new body.

HOW TO USE THIS BOOK 11

BUG SPOTTING

Follow these simple steps and you will be an expert bug spotter in no time.

1. Start by looking up your favorite bug in the index on page 174.
2. Look at the detailed artwork. Arrows point to special features.
3. Look out for extra facts in the colored circles. There are IT'S WILD! facts at the bottom of the pages, too.

SPOTTER FACT

Locusts cause famines. Scientists are finding environmentally friendly ways to stop locusts destroying crops.

There are no physical differences between a grasshopper and a locust. The name changes when they gather together in groups.

WHERE IN THE WORLD?

LIVES: farmland, sand dunes, Central and South America, Africa, Asia, Australia, Europe
EATS: plants
STATUS:
- least concern

HOW BIG?

female 2–2.7in (5–7cm) long;
male 1.2–1.7in (3–4.5cm) long

4. Find your bearings on the world map. See where the bugs live and in what kind of habitat.
5. Bugs are hard to study, so we don't always know if they are in danger. Check here to see whether their conservation status has been assessed.
6. Compare the size of the bug with the size of a person.

Locust

IT'S WILD! Bugs are arthropods—the largest group in the animal kingdom. They make up more than 80 percent of all known animal species.

BUTTERFLIES

AND MOTHS

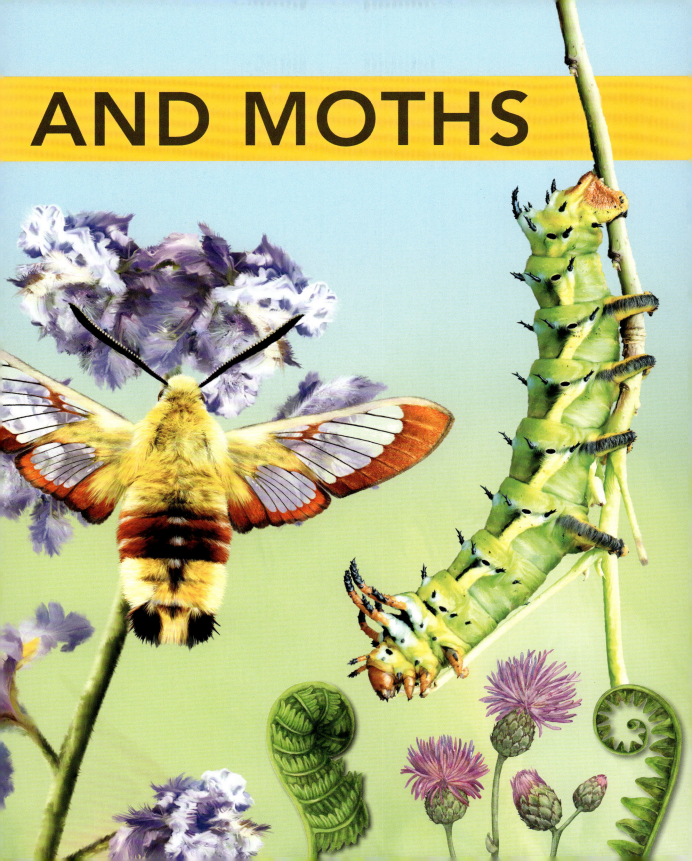

14 SPOTTER'S GUIDE BUTTERFLIES AND MOTHS

HOW TO SPOT BUTTERFLIES AND MOTHS

Whether fluttering around in the air or resting on a plant, butterflies and moths are sure to catch your eye. These delicate insects belong to the group Lepidoptera. They can be brightly colored or superbly camouflaged and are found deep in the rainforest, in flower-filled meadows, or in your backyard or local park.

BUTTERFLY AND MOTH WATCH

Imagine coming across a beautiful butterfly flying around on a summer's day. Watch it settle on a plant to feed or lay eggs. Take note of its colors and patterns so that you can look it up later.

LOOK ALL AROUND
In the daytime, you're more likely to spot a butterfly than a moth. You'll find them feeding on flower nectar or fruit, or clustering around muddy puddles, drinking up the salt.

Above and below
The top side of the wings can be different from the underside. Bright colors warn off predators.

Look at the antennae
Thin antennae that end in little clubs mean the insect is a butterfly.

Look at the legs
Some butterflies appear to have four legs rather than six because the front pair are smaller.

Orange oakleaf butterfly

Clever camouflage
The brown, mottled colors of the undersides of the wings help the butterfly to camouflage among dead leaves.

BUTTERFLIES AND MOTHS SPOTTER'S GUIDE

HOW DO BUTTERFLIES AND MOTHS LIVE?

Butterflies are active during the day. Moths generally come out at night. Their caterpillars often feed on just one or two types of plant, so the female will lay her eggs there.

Puss moth caterpillar

CRAZY CATERPILLARS
Caterpillars have clever ways to protect themselves. The puss moth caterpillar makes itself look terrifying by shaking its hind "tails."

Polyphemus moth

WHAT MAKES A BUTTERFLY AND A MOTH?

Scaly wings: Butterflies and moths are the only insects that have scales covering their wings.

Colors: Butterflies are usually more colorful than moths. Moths are often dull in color with furry bodies—although there are many exceptions.

Antennae: Butterfly antennae are thin and have a slightly thicker end, like a club. Moth antennae are feathery or threadlike.

Larvae: Butterfly and moth larvae are called caterpillars. They have three pairs of true legs under the thorax. There are also four pairs of fleshy prolegs on the abdomen, which they use to grip onto plants and shuffle forward.

FALSE EYES
Butterflies and moths sometimes have markings that look like the eyes of a bigger, more dangerous creature.

STAY AWAY!
The postman butterfly's striking colors tell predators that it is poisonous. Other creatures will leave it alone.

Postman butterfly

SPOTTER'S GUIDE: BUTTERFLIES AND MOTHS

AMERICAN SNOUT

This curious butterfly is named after its long mouthparts, which look like a pointy snout. After heavy summer rains, millions of snout butterflies fly together to look for fresh food and mates.

American snout

This butterfly turns from an egg to an adult in just two weeks.

WHERE IN THE WORLD?

LIVES: deciduous woodland, gardens, North, Central, and South America
EATS: rotting fruit, flower nectar
STATUS: least concern

HOW BIG?
1.4–2in (3.5–5cm) wingspan

GLASSWING

WHERE IN THE WORLD?

LIVES: rainforests, Central and South America, southern US
EATS: flower nectar, bird droppings

HOW BIG?
2.2–2.4in (5.6–6.1cm) wingspan

This butterfly is hard to spot in the gloom of the rainforest because its wings are almost completely see-through, like glass. It might look delicate, but the glasswing is a powerful flier.

Glasswing

Glasswings travel up to 12 miles (20km) per day.

BUTTERFLIES AND MOTHS SPOTTER'S GUIDE   17

PAPER KITE

WHERE IN THE WORLD?

LIVES: rainforest, mangrove swamps, East and Southeast Asia
EATS: flower nectar

HOW BIG?
4.5–5.5in (12–14cm) wingspan

What's that wafting around the rainforest like a large piece of paper? You've spotted a paper kite butterfly jerkily fluttering about like a kite!

Paper kite

Unusually for butterflies, the paper kite rests with its wings open.

PAINTED LADY

WHERE IN THE WORLD?

LIVES: meadows, fields, parks, marshes, scrubland, sand dunes, mountains, Africa, Asia, Europe, North and Central America
EATS: flower nectar
STATUS:
 least concern

HOW BIG?
2–2.7in (5–7cm) wingspan

WHOOSH! A painted lady butterfly has just zipped past. It's one of the fastest fliers, reaching speeds of 30mph (50km/h).

The butterfly can travel 100 miles (160km) in a single day.

Painted lady

SPOTTER'S GUIDE BUTTERFLIES AND MOTHS

RED CRACKER

Look on tree trunks to find this butterfly. The male rests head down, which tells the females he is looking for a mate.

Red cracker

This butterfly is named after the undersides of its wings, which are red.

WHERE IN THE WORLD?

LIVES: rainforests, dry forests, Central and South America, southern US
EATS: rotting fruit, animal dung

HOW BIG?
3–3.4in (7.4–8.6cm) wingspan

TAWNY COSTER

Meet the butterfly world's long-distance flier! The tawny coster has been known to fly more than 400 miles (700km) across the sea from Indonesia to Australia without stopping.

The female lays twenty to a hundred yellow eggs at a time.

Tawny coster

WHERE IN THE WORLD?

LIVES: grassland, scrubland, woodland, parks, roadsides, India, Sri Lanka, Southeast Asia, Australia
EATS: flower nectar

HOW BIG?
1.6–2.5in (4–6.4cm) wingspan

BUTTERFLIES AND MOTHS **SPOTTER'S GUIDE** 19

ORANGE OAKLEAF

Watch where you step! The orange oakleaf butterfly looks like a dead leaf when its wings are closed—perfect for hiding in the leaf litter on the forest floor.

WHERE IN THE WORLD?

LIVES: tropical forests, mountain forests, East and South Asia
EATS: rotting fruit, tree sap, dung

HOW BIG?

3.3–4.3in (8.5–11cm) wingspan

These butterflies drink from muddy puddles. The water contains nutrious mineral salts.

Orange oakleaf

POSTMAN

WHERE IN THE WORLD?

LIVES: forests, Central and South America
EATS: pollen, flower nectar, ripe or rotting fruit

HOW BIG?

2.5–3.3in (6.4–8.4cm) wingspan

By day, postman butterflies fly slowly from flower to flower, always using the same route. Creep through the forests at night to see large groups resting together for safety.

The black and red colors tell predators that the butterfly is poisonous.

Postman

MONARCH

If you look up at the skies in autumn in North America, you'll witness one of nature's most spectacular events. Swarms of monarch butterflies fly from chilly Canada to spend the winter in Mexico, where the weather is much warmer. That's a distance of 3,000 miles (5,000km)—a long way for a butterfly to fly!

Scientists think the antennae help the butterflies know when to migrate.

Monarch

DON'T MISS!
Look for oyamel fir trees in Mexican forests. Monarchs roost in them in their thousands, almost without moving.

Monarchs migrate in the day and rest at night.

The strong wings flap five to twelve times per second, much slower than the normal twenty times per second.

BUTTERFLIES AND MOTHS **SPOTTER'S GUIDE** **21**

WHERE IN THE WORLD?

LIVES: fields, forests, gardens, parks, roadsides, North America

EATS: milkweed leaves (caterpillar); flower nectar (butterfly)

STATUS:
vulnerable

HOW BIG?
4in (10cm) wingspan

The chrysalis becomes see-through after the butterfly emerges.

IN DANGER
The monarch is endangered. Planting milkweed, the caterpillar's favorite food, will help it to survive.

HATCHING OUT
The monarch changes from caterpillar to butterfly inside a case called a chrysalis. When it emerges, the butterfly's wings are wet and creased. To get ready for flight, the monarch pumps fluid and air through the veins to stretch the wings out and waits for them to dry off.

SPOTTER'S GUIDE BUTTERFLIES AND MOTHS

BALTIMORE CHECKERSPOT

WHERE IN THE WORLD?

LIVES: wet meadows, bogs, marshes, grassland, wooded hillsides, dry fields, North America
EATS: flower nectar, dung, dead animals
STATUS: endangered

HOW BIG?
1.7–2.7in (4.5–7cm) wingspan

The black and orange colors of this rare butterfly make it easy to spot in the countryside. They are also a signal that the butterfly tastes bad.

The butterfly spreads its wings while feeding to show off its warning colors.

Baltimore checkerspot

CLEOPATRA

WHERE IN THE WORLD?

LIVES: open woodland, scrubland, mountains, gardens, North Africa, Mediterranean Europe, Middle East
EATS: flower nectar

HOW BIG?
2–2.7in (5–7cm) wingspan

The Cleopatra belongs to a family of butterflies that have white, yellow, or orange colors. These come from the waste products in the insects' bodies.

The veins and brown spots on the undersides of the wings make the butterfly look like a dying leaf.

Cleopatra

BUTTERFLIES AND MOTHS **SPOTTER'S GUIDE**

APOLLO

When searching for this butterfly, make sure you're well wrapped up—the Apollo lives in cold climates. It is named after the ancient Greek sun god, who was considered the most beautiful god.

WHERE IN THE WORLD?

LIVES: mountains, grassland and rocky slopes, forests, Europe, Central Asia
EATS: flower nectar
STATUS:
🍃 least concern

HOW BIG?

2.5–9.5in (6.2–9.5cm) wingspan

The red eyespots scare off predators and protect the butterfly's real eyes from being eaten by birds.

Apollo

CAIRNS BIRDWING

WHERE IN THE WORLD?

LIVES: rainforests, gardens, Queensland in Australia
EATS: flower nectar, rotting fruit
STATUS:
🍃 least concern

HOW BIG?

females 6in (15cm); males 5in (13cm) wingspan

Meet Australia's butterfly giant! Not reflected under How Big? section, the Cairns birdwing is mighty enough to chase off birds from its territory.

Cairns birdwing

The male shows off his bright colors to the female to encourage her to mate.

24 SPOTTER'S GUIDE BUTTERFLIES AND MOTHS

SWALLOWTAILS

These butterflies get their name from the long "tails" on their hindwings that look like a swallow's tail. Large and colorful, swallowtails can be found all over the world, with many living in tropical climates.

SPOTTER FACT

Swallowtails have many predators. Common ones include birds, skink lizards, skunks, fireflies, mantises, and spiders.

The anise swallowtail has a much shorter body than the similar-looking Canadian tiger swallowtail.

Anise swallowtail

This species lives in cold climates. It has chemicals in its body to stop it from freezing.

Canadian tiger swallowtail

Pipevine swallowtail

The female pipevine swallowtail is duller than the male, which has shiny blue colors on its hindwings.

BUTTERFLIES AND MOTHS SPOTTER'S GUIDE 25

Orchard swallowtail

Although it is part of the swallowtail family, the orchard swallowtail doesn't have long tails at the rear.

Giant swallowtail caterpillar

CLEVER DISGUISE
The caterpillar of the giant swallowtail butterfly looks like a bird dropping. This incredible camouflage means the caterpillar can rest in plain sight, safe from predators.

WHERE IN THE WORLD?

LIVES: woodland, grassland, meadows, gardens
- Canadian tiger swallowtail: Canada, northern US
- Pipevine swallowtail: North and Central America
- Anise swallowtail: North America
- Orchard swallowtail: Australia, Papua New Guinea
- Giant swallowtail: US, Mexico, Cuba

EATS: citrus leaves, carrot leaves, deciduous tree leaves, pipevine (caterpillar); flower nectar (butterfly)

STATUS:
Pipevine swallowtail, Anise swallowtail, and Giant swallowtail—least concern

HOW BIG?

 Canadian tiger swallowtail 2.5–3in (6.4–8cm) wingspan

 Pipevine swallowtail 2.7–5in (7–13cm) wingspan

 Anise swallowtail 2–3in (5.2–8cm) wingspan

 Orchard swallowtail 1.8–2.2in (4.7–5.5cm) wingspan

 Giant swallowtail caterpillar up to 2in (5cm) long

26 SPOTTER'S GUIDE BUTTERFLIES AND MOTHS

PEACOCK

WHERE IN THE WORLD?

LIVES: woodland, fields, meadows, gardens, parks, mountains, Europe, Asia

EATS: nettle leaves (caterpillar); flower nectar, tree sap, rotten fruit (butterfly)

STATUS:
 least concern

HOW BIG?

caterpillar 1.5in (3.8cm) long; 2.2–2.5in (5.7–6.4cm) wingspan

What's that strange noise? When threatened, peacock butterflies rub their wings together to make a hissing sound. The noise can scare predators like mice and birds away. If that doesn't work, the butterflies spread out their wings to show four large eyespots. These make them look like a bigger, scarier animal.

The eyespots look like the markings on peacock feathers. They give this butterfly its name.

Peacock

SAFETY IN NUMBERS

When they are two weeks old, peacock butterfly caterpillars get together and spin a silk web. They all live and feed inside the web for safety.

Peacock butterfly caterpillar

Peacock caterpillars are covered in spikes, which helps protect them from predators.

BUTTERFLIES AND MOTHS **SPOTTER'S GUIDE** 27

GREEN HAIRSTREAK

Hairstreak butterflies are named for the hairlike streak across the undersides of their wings. The tops of the green hairstreak's wings are brown, so you only see its bright green color when it's resting.

Green hairstreak

The green hairstreak has a row of white dots as its "streak."

WHERE IN THE WORLD?

LIVES: grassland, woodland, heathland, moorland, wetlands, Europe, North Africa, Asia
EATS: flower nectar
STATUS:
🍃 least concern

HOW BIG?

1–1.2in (2.6–3cm) wingspan

LONG-TAILED SKIPPER

WHERE IN THE WORLD?

LIVES: fields, meadows, woodland, gardens, roadsides, coastal dunes, Central and South America, southern and eastern US
EATS: flower nectar

HOW BIG?

1.7–2.3in (4.5–6cm) wingspan

Skippers get their name from the jerky way they fly, skipping between flowers rather than gliding smoothly like a typical butterfly.

A skipper's antennae are hooked at the end.

The back wings are extended so that they look like two long tails.

Long-tailed skipper

SPOTTER'S GUIDE: BUTTERFLIES AND MOTHS

This species is also known as the American moon moth. Scientists think its long wing tails confuse the echolocation of its main predator—bats.

SPOTTER FACT
New adults emerge from pupas in the morning. This allows their wings to dry before their first night flight.

MOON MOTHS

Large and graceful moon moths get their name from the white eyespots on their wings that are shaped like crescent moons. You'll need the Moon's bright light to see them, as they fly around at night.

Luna moth

The Spanish moon moth lives in mountainous areas and can survive very low temperatures.

IN DANGER
Spanish moon moths are threatened by climate change and pesticide use. In some countries, they are protected by law.

Spanish moon moth

BUTTERFLIES AND MOTHS SPOTTER'S GUIDE

The female lays her eggs on leaves.

The caterpillar makes silk, which it wraps around itself to make a tough cocoon. This protects the pupa while it changes into its adult form.

The adult moth emerges from the cocoon.

The Indian moon moth prefers warm and humid climates.

Indian moon moth

MUNCHING CATERPILLARS

Adult moon moths don't eat during their short lives. They survive on the energy that the caterpillar stored up by eating leaves. These massive munchers increase their weight more than four thousand times before they become a pupa.

WHERE IN THE WORLD?

LIVES: dry mountain pine forests, deciduous forests, tropical forests

- Spanish moon moth: Spain, France, Switzerland
- Luna moth: North America
- Indian moon moth: Asia

EATS: tree leaves (caterpillar); no food (moth)

STATUS:
  Spanish moon moth—endangered

HOW BIG?

Spanish moon moth 2.3–4in (6–10cm) wingspan

Luna moth 3–4.5in (8–12cm) wingspan

Indian moon moth 5–7in (13–17cm) wingspan

HERCULES MOTH

This enormous moth is the largest in Australia. It is named after the mythical ancient Roman hero Hercules, who was known for his great strength.

Viewed from the side, the moth's wing tips look like the head of a snake.

Hercules moth

WHERE IN THE WORLD?

LIVES: rainforests, northern Australia, New Guinea
EATS: no food

HOW BIG?

10.5–11.8in (27–30cm) wingspan

MADAGASCAN SUNSET MOTH

WHERE IN THE WORLD?

LIVES: deciduous forests, rainforests, Madagascar
EATS: flower nectar

HOW BIG?

2.7–4.3in (7–11cm) wingspan

You don't have to stay up late to spot this moth—it flies around during the day. Admire its gorgeous colors, which look like the sky when the Sun is setting.

Madagascan sunset moth

The moth is toxic to predators because of the plants their caterpillars eat.

LOBSTER MOTH

The lobster moth is rather ordinary-looking, but wait until you see its caterpillar. This curious creature is able to arch its head and bottom over its back until it looks just like a miniature lobster! It does this when threatened by predators.

The wings are grayish-brown and give the moth good camouflage against tree bark.

Lobster moth

WHERE IN THE WORLD?

LIVES: deciduous woodland, Europe, Asia
EATS: leaves of oak, beech, birch, hazel, chestnut, and other trees (caterpillar); flower nectar (moth)

HOW BIG?

caterpillar 2.7in (7cm) long; moth 1.6–2.7in (4–7cm) wingspan

Its furry body protects it from hungry birds, which struggle to swallow hair.

The caterpillar can squirt acid from its tail to fend off attackers, such as squirrels.

Lobster moth caterpillar

SPOTTER FACT
When bred in captivity, lobster caterpillars fight with each other. They have to be kept separate for their safety.

SCARING OFF
The lobster caterpillar does its best to make itself look unappealing to attackers. The thorn-shaped bumps on its back make it seem too tough to eat. When curled into its "lobster" pose, the caterpillar waves its legs and two "tails" so that it resembles a dangerous scorpion or spider.

HAWK MOTHS

Hawk moths can look quite different from one another, but they always have a thick, hairy body that is pointed at each end. Some have such amazing colors and shapes that they look like another creature entirely.

This species is sometimes called the army green moth because it has camouflage patterns like a soldier's uniform.

Powerful wings mean the moth can fly up to 12mph (20km/h).

Oleander hawk moth

Broad-bordered bee hawk moth

Thick brown bands, or borders, on the wings give this hawk moth its name.

The broad-bordered bee hawk moth could be mistaken for a bumblebee. This protects it from predators.

WHERE IN THE WORLD?

LIVES: woodland, heathland, grassland, scrubland, forests, deserts, parks, gardens
- Oleander hawk moth: Africa, Asia, Europe, Hawaii
- Broad-bordered bee hawk moth: Europe, Asia

EATS: flower nectar

HOW BIG?

Oleander hawk moth 3.5–5in (9–13cm) wingspan

Broad-bordered bee hawk moth 1.5–1.9in (3.8–4.8cm) wingspan

BUTTERFLIES AND MOTHS **SPOTTER'S GUIDE** 33

WHERE IN THE WORLD?

LIVES: woodland, scrubland, gardens, parks, North, Central, and South America
EATS: no food

HOW BIG?
female 2in (5cm);
male 3.5in (9cm) wingspan

GIANT LEOPARD MOTH

You'll know the giant leopard moth from its spots. These look like the markings of a snow leopard.

The moth lives for just a few days, but its caterpillar can live for as long as three years.

Giant leopard moth

VAMPIRE MOTH

The vampire moth gets its name because it feeds on mammal blood—even yours! This won't harm you, but you might feel a little sting. It's better to keep your distance.

WHERE IN THE WORLD?

LIVES: forests, grassland, scrubland, North America, South and Southeast Asia, Australia
EATS: fruit, flower nectar, mammal blood

HOW BIG?
up to 1.5in (3.8cm) wingspan

Its camouflage makes this moth look like a dead leaf.

Vampire moth

SPOTTER'S GUIDE — BUTTERFLIES AND MOTHS

CINNABAR MOTH

This brightly colored moth is named after the mineral cinnabar, which artists once used to make red paint. See it fluttering around in the daytime.

The cinnabar moth is poisonous. The toxins come from the ragwort plant that the caterpillars eat.

Cinnabar moth

WHERE IN THE WORLD?

LIVES: grassland, sand dunes, heathland, gardens, farmland, woodland, Europe, Asia, New Zealand, Australia, North America

EATS: ragwort (caterpillar); flower nectar (butterfly)

HOW BIG?

1.3–1.6in (3.2–4.2cm) wingspan

PEPPERED MOTH

With its salt-and-pepper coloring, the peppered moth is brilliantly camouflaged against mossy bark. Look closely at tree trunks to find it resting during the day.

The comblike antennae detect smells in the air, helping the moth find food.

Peppered moth

WHERE IN THE WORLD?

LIVES: woodland, meadows, scrubland, hedgerows, parks, gardens, Europe, North America, Asia

EATS: flower nectar, rotting fruit

HOW BIG?

1.7–2.4in (4.5–6.2cm) wingspan

BUTTERFLIES AND MOTHS **SPOTTER'S GUIDE** 35

WHERE IN THE WORLD?

LIVES: woodland, parks, eastern US, southern Canada
EATS: no food

HOW BIG?

1.3–2.2in (3.2–5.5cm) wingspan

ROSY MAPLE MOTH

The rosy maple is the smallest of the silk moths. Look for it in the daytime among the leaves of maple trees or watch it flying around at night.

Its bright colors give the moth good camouflage in the pinkish maple leaves.

Rosy maple moth

WHERE IN THE WORLD?

LIVES: woodland, fields, eastern US, Canada, Mexico
EATS: flower nectar

HOW BIG?

1–1.5in (2.5–3.8cm) wingspan

EIGHT-SPOTTED FORESTER

Don't mistake this moth for a butterfly, even though it sips flower nectar and flies in the daytime like butterflies do. Its hairy body will tell you that it's a moth.

When its wings are fully open, you can see the eight white spots that give the moth its name.

Eight-spotted forester

SPOTTER'S GUIDE — BUTTERFLIES AND MOTHS

POLYPHEMUS MOTH

Two large eyes peer at you out of the gloom. Don't be afraid! It's not a dangerous animal, just the Polyphemus moth trying to scare off predators with its two large eyespots. These false eyes—one in the middle of each hindwing—give this enormous silk moth its name. Polyphemus was a mythical ancient Greek giant who had one eye in the center of his forehead.

SPOTTER FACT
This caterpillar eats leaves from more than fifty types of tree. Most other caterpillars eat just one type.

The moth has no need for any working mouthparts.

The moth spreads out its forewings to flash its false eyes at attackers, such as squirrels.

Polyphemus moths live for less than a week.

The markings make the hindwings look like the head of the great horned owl, a skillful hunter.

Polyphemus moth

WHERE IN THE WORLD?

LIVES: deciduous woodland, wetlands, parks, fields, gardens, Canada, US, Mexico
EATS: leaves such as birch, oak, maple, willow, walnut, fruit trees (caterpillar); no food (moth)
STATUS: least concern

HOW BIG?

caterpillar 2.3–3in (6–7.5cm) long; moth 4–6in (10–15cm) wingspan

CHANGING COLORS
Caterpillars have several stages of growth and can look quite different each time. At first, the Polyphemus moth caterpillar is white with black stripes and spiky orange hairs. In its final stage, it becomes bright green.

The caterpillar can eat 86,000 times its body weight in less than two months.

Polyphemus moth caterpillar

BUTTERFLIES AND MOTHS **SPOTTER'S GUIDE** 37

GARDEN TIGER MOTH

If you're romping over sand dunes or walking anywhere in the countryside in the evening, you're likely to spot this very common moth. When its wings are closed, you can see just a furry brown head and brown-and-white patterned wings. When the wings are open, the moth's bright orange body and hindwings are revealed.

WHERE IN THE WORLD?

LIVES: grassland, meadows, gardens, woodland, sand dunes, North America, Europe, Asia

EATS: leaves of nettle, thistle, willowherb, dock, plantain, foxglove, fungi, dead animals (caterpillar); flower nectar (moth)

HOW BIG?

caterpillar 1.6–2.3in (4–6cm) long; moth 1.6–3in (4–7.6cm) wingspan

The orange color and black spots show that the moth is poisonous to eat.

The female picks several different types of plant to lay her eggs on.

Garden tiger moth

The hairs contain formic acid and can give people a skin rash.

WOOLLY BEARS

The garden tiger moth caterpillar is covered in long, spiky hairs. These kinds of caterpillars are sometimes called woolly bears. The furry covering keeps the garden tiger caterpillar warm when it hibernates through the winter.

Garden tiger moth caterpillar

IT'S WILD! A flash of its bright orange colors is enough to startle a predator, giving the moth time to escape.

SPOTTER'S GUIDE: BUTTERFLIES AND MOTHS

WHERE IN THE WORLD?

LIVES: deciduous woodland, eastern US

EATS: leaves of walnut, hickory, sweet gum, persimmon, sumac (caterpillar); no food (moth)

HOW BIG?

caterpillar 5–6in (12.5–15cm) long; moth 3.7–6in (9.5–15cm) wingspan

REGAL MOTH

Stunning reddish-brown colors give the regal moth its other name—the royal walnut moth. It's one of the heaviest moths, mainly because its enormous caterpillar eats so much before it turns into a pupa. Despite its great weight, the male can fly for miles to find a mate.

When it is ready to turn into a pupa, this species makes a burrow in the ground rather than spinning a cocoon.

The nut-brown wings have several yellow spots.

Regal moth

Regal moth caterpillar

HICKORY HORNED DEVIL
The regal moth caterpillar is a whopping creature. Long and heavy bodied, it is known as the hickory horned devil because of the hickory tree leaves it loves to eat. It also has two spiky horns on its head, like a devil.

The male mates with several different females.

IT'S WILD! The moth lives for only a week. It must mate and lay eggs in this short time.

PUSS MOTH

The puss moth is covered in so much fluffy hair that it was named after a cat. It's quite easy to identify because of the black and gray marble patterns that cover its white body and wings. You'll see it flying around at night in spring and summer.

WHERE IN THE WORLD?

LIVES: woodland, parks, gardens, Europe, Asia
EATS: willow and poplar leaves (caterpillar); no food (moth)

HOW BIG?

caterpillar 2.2–3in (6–8cm) long; moth 2.25–3in (6–8cm) wingspan

Puss moth

The large antennae are feathery.

The puss moth belongs to the family of silk moths.

Puss moth caterpillar

The dark saddle on its back helps to disguise the caterpillars shape among the leaves.

MASTER OF DISGUISE

The puss moth caterpillar has a pink "face" with two false eyes on the top of its head. When it feels threatened, it shows off its face and waves the two long "tails" on its rear.

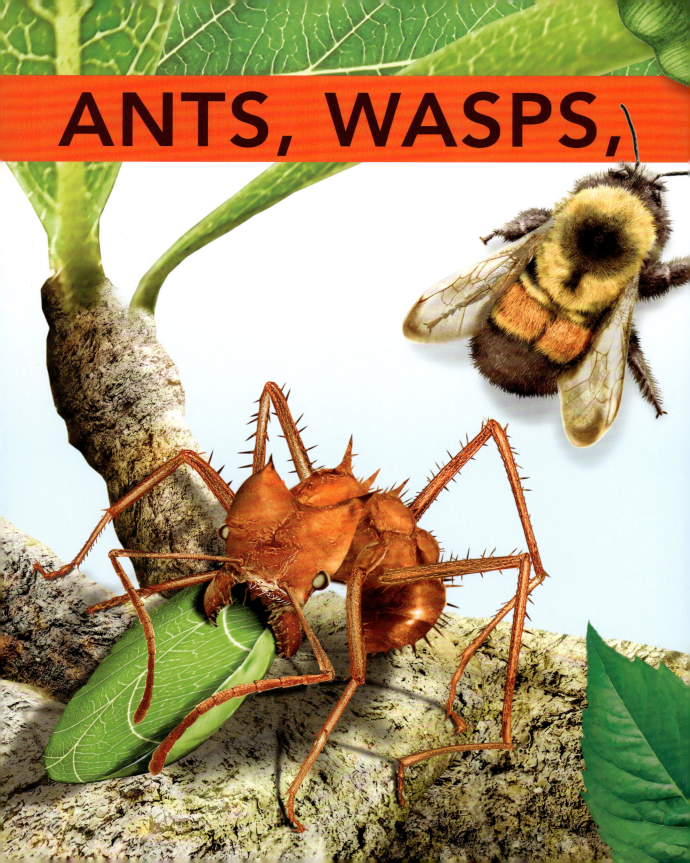

ANTS, WASPS,

AND BEES

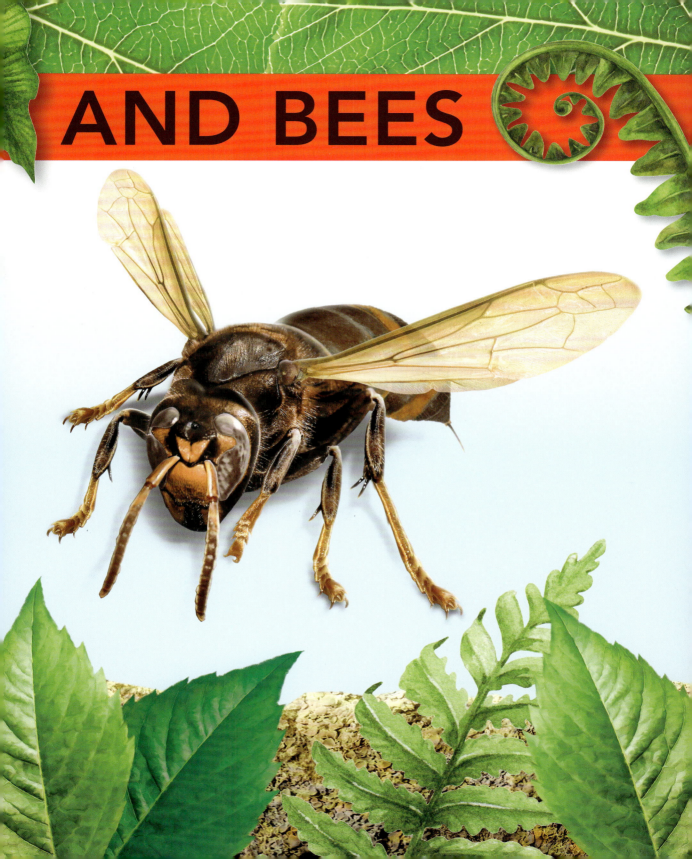

42 SPOTTER'S GUIDE ANTS, WASPS, AND BEES

HOW TO SPOT ANTS, WASPS, AND BEES

Look and listen! A bee buzzes, a wasp scratches, and a line of ants marches. These insects are quite different from one another, but all belong to the order, or group, called Hymenoptera. This huge collection of insects includes the smallest of them all—the fairy fly.

ANT, WASP, AND BEE WATCH
Imagine zooming in with your binoculars to examine ants, wasps, and bees at work. See if you can spot the jobs they do, whether it's building a nest, feeding their young, or making honey.

LOOK DOWN
When exploring, look for ants at your feet or in trees. Wasps often nest in the ground, and bees can usually be seen buzzing around flowers.

Spot the key feature
Look for the most obvious feature to help identify a member of this group. Wasps usually have a shiny rather than hairy body.

Examine the wings
Wings are see-through with very few veins.

What does it eat?
Some bugs from this group are plant eaters, while others are meat eaters. Wasps often eat both.

Social or solitary?
See if the bug is on its own or with others of its kind. Some types of wasp live alone. Others live in colonies.

Nasonia jewel wasp

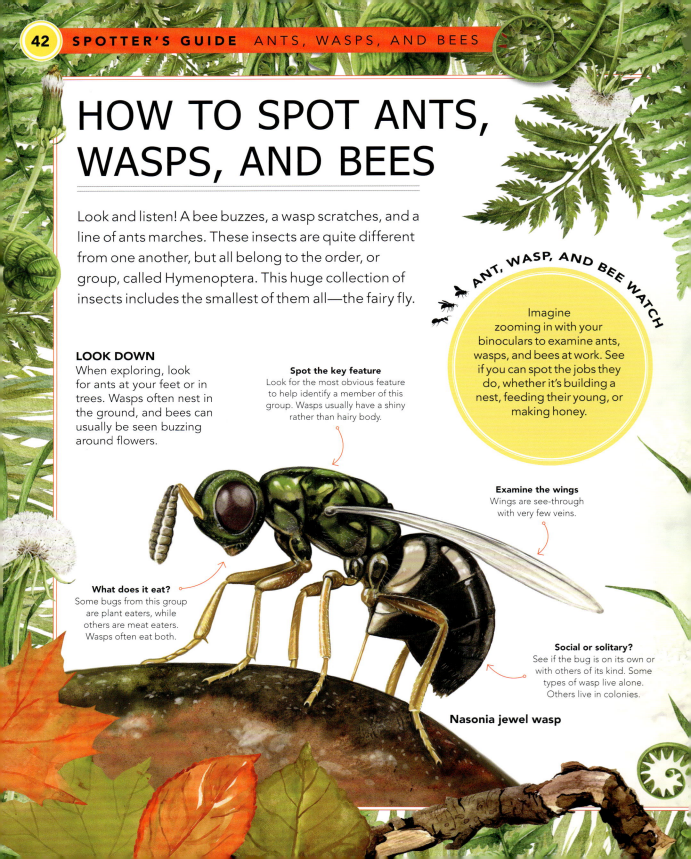

ANTS, WASPS, AND BEES **SPOTTER'S GUIDE** 43

HOW DO ANTS, WASPS, AND BEES LIVE?

Like all insects, ants, wasps, and bees have to protect themselves. Ants bite and spray acid at predators. Wasps and bees can sting. They only do so if provoked.

ODD SHAPES
Some wasps develop inside strangely shaped growths called galls. These provide a covering for the larva and pupa as they grow.

Gall wasp

Pharoah ant

LIVING TOGETHER
Ants and some wasps and bees live in large colonies, or groups. There are workers and queens, each with their own job to do.

HELPFUL POLLINATOR
When a bee visits a flower, pollen sticks to its body. This rubs off on the next flower the bee flies to. The flower can then make seeds.

Rusty-patched bumblebee

WHAT MAKES AN ANT, A WASP, AND A BEE?

Narrow waist: The thorax and abdomen of ants, wasps, and bees are separated by a "waist." The exception is sawflies, which have no waist.

Joined wings: Wasps, bees, and flying ants have two pairs of wings that are linked with hooks. The forewings are larger than the hindwings.

Biting jaws: Members of this group have mouthparts that can bite and chew. Most bees also have a long tube called a proboscis for sucking up nectar.

Egg laying: Females have a long, thin tube called an ovipositor for laying eggs. In some species, the ovipositor is modified to sting.

44 SPOTTER'S GUIDE: ANTS, WASPS, AND BEES

LEAFCUTTER ANT

Look up to see a parade of leafcutter ants marching along a branch. They have nibbled off pieces of leaf from the tree and are carrying them back to their nest on the ground. The ants will use the leaves to make compost for growing the fungus they eat.

WHERE IN THE WORLD?

LIVES: tropical forests, farmland, plantations, Central and South America, Mexico

EATS: fungus, plant sap

HOW BIG?

0.1–0.9in (0.2–2.3cm) long

SPOTTER FACT

Ants' nests can be nearly 500 feet wide and contain around eight million ants. Some colonies survive for eight years.

An ant can carry up to fifty times its own body weight.

Ants have sticky pads and curved claws on their legs to help them grip vertical tree trunks.

Leafcutter ants use their sharp, scissorlike jaws to nibble off pieces of leaf.

Leafcutter ant

ANTS, WASPS, AND BEES **SPOTTER'S GUIDE** 45

HONEYPOT ANT

Search around the bottom of a plant or in a clump of grass and you may see an ant that looks like it's carrying a huge globule of honey. You've found the entrance to a honeypot ant nest. This ant uses its own body as a store cupboard for honey to eat when food is scarce.

When other ants are hungry, they stroke the antennae of the huge-bellied ant. This causes it to spit out the honey.

Honeypot ant

The ant's abdomen swells up to several times its normal size to hold all the honey.

The ants become so big that moving is difficult. They hang from the roof of the nest and are fed by other ants.

WHERE IN THE WORLD?

LIVES: scrubland, grassland, North America, Australia
EATS: honeydew, flower nectar, seeds, termites

HOW BIG?

up to 1.2in (3cm) long

IT'S WILD!   Indigenous people in North America and Australia eat honeypot ants. They are considered a delicacy.

46 SPOTTER'S GUIDE ANTS, WASPS, AND BEES

SIAFU ANT

These ferocious ants will attack anything—and anyone—that crosses their path. You'll see huge columns of them on the ground, marching in a long line like soldiers.

When these ants are on the move, twenty million of them can travel together at a time.

Siafu ant

WHERE IN THE WORLD?

LIVES: rainforests, savannas, Africa, South and Southeast Asia
EATS: insects, dead animals

HOW BIG?

up to 2.5in (6.3cm) long

PHARAOH ANT

WHERE IN THE WORLD?

LIVES: in buildings worldwide
EATS: human food and food waste, dead animals, other insects

HOW BIG?

up to 0.2in (0.5cm) long

These yellowish-brown ants live in colonies in dark corners of buildings. Pharaoh ants might even be in your home because they love to feast on human food!

Pharaoh ants need warmth. They live in buildings when it's cold outside.

Pharoah ant

ANTS, WASPS, AND BEES **SPOTTER'S GUIDE** 47

EUROPEAN WASP

WHERE IN THE WORLD?

LIVES: grassland, urban, Europe, northern Africa, introduced worldwide
EATS: dead animals, spiders, fruit, honeydew, human food

HOW BIG?
0.5in (1.3cm) long

If you listen carefully, you might hear a scratching sound. That's a wasp chewing off wood from trees, fences, and sheds. It uses the wood fibers to build its underground nest.

This is a social wasp. These types of wasps live in colonies with other wasps rather than on their own.

European wasp

ASIAN GIANT HORNET

WHERE IN THE WORLD?

LIVES: lowland mountains and forests, East and Southeast Asia
EATS: bees, mantises, beetles, other hornets, tree sap

HOW BIG?
1.4–2in (3.5–5cm) long

A hornet is a type of wasp. Asian giant hornets are vicious predators. They can destroy a whole honey bee colony in just a few hours.

The Asian giant hornet has an orange head. Other types of hornet have yellow heads.

Asian giant hornet

48 SPOTTER'S GUIDE ANTS, WASPS, AND BEES

SOLITARY WASPS

Solitary wasps live alone rather than in colonies. They are predators, hunting and capturing other insects or spiders to feed to their larvae. Solitary wasps usually have smooth, shiny bodies with very few hairs. They can sting, but if left alone, they are rarely aggressive to people.

SPOTTER FACT
People used to call red velvet ants cowkillers. They mistakenly thought their sting was strong enough to kill a cow.

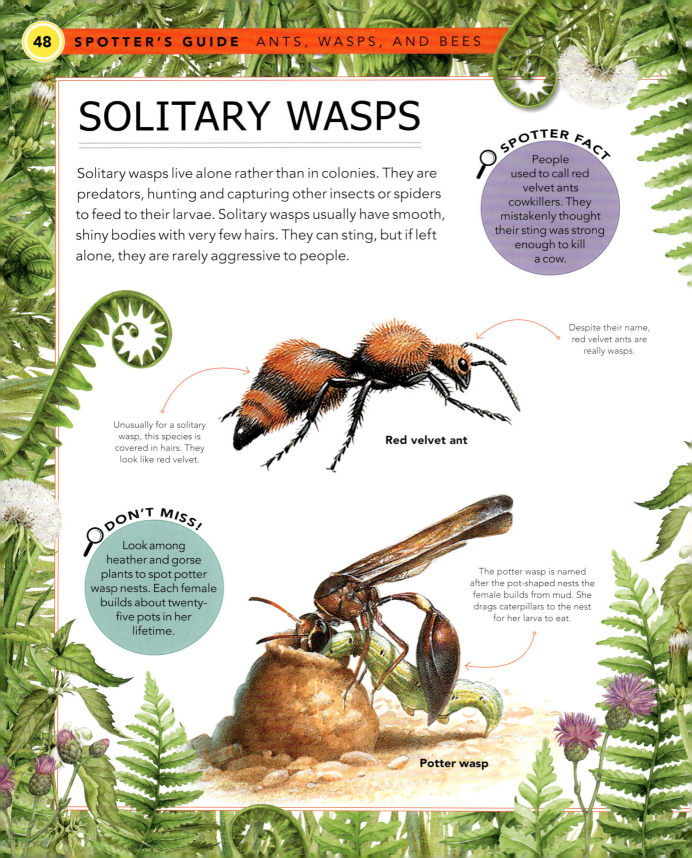

Unusually for a solitary wasp, this species is covered in hairs. They look like red velvet.

Despite their name, red velvet ants are really wasps.

Red velvet ant

DON'T MISS!
Look among heather and gorse plants to spot potter wasp nests. Each female builds about twenty-five pots in her lifetime.

The potter wasp is named after the pot-shaped nests the female builds from mud. She drags caterpillars to the nest for her larva to eat.

Potter wasp

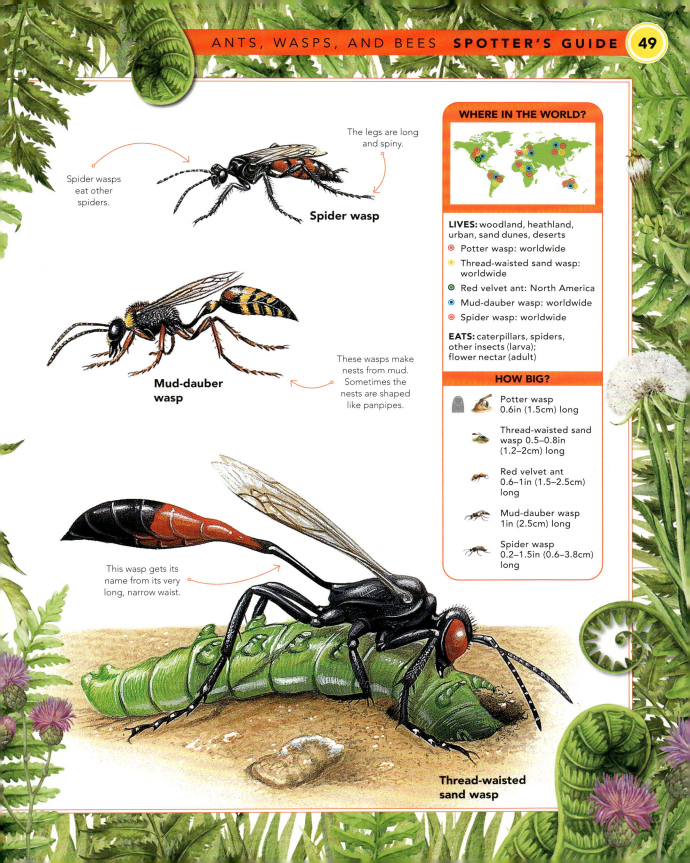

SPOTTER'S GUIDE ANTS, WASPS, AND BEES

PARASITIC WASPS

Many types of wasp are parasites. These include a group of tiny, metallic-colored wasps called chalcid wasps. Parasitic wasps lay their eggs in the bodies of other creatures, which are known as the hosts. When the larva hatches from the egg, it feasts on the live host until it is big enough to change into an adult. The host creature is left to die.

Eulophid wasp

This species of chalcid wasp seeks out a host moth called a citrus leafminer.

Sabre wasp

Sabre wasps use wood-boring larvae as their hosts. To get to a larva, the wasps have to drill through the wood first.

SPOTTER FACT

The sabre wasp is a type of ichneumon wasp. This is one of the biggest families in the animal kingdom.

ANTS, WASPS, AND BEES SPOTTER'S GUIDE

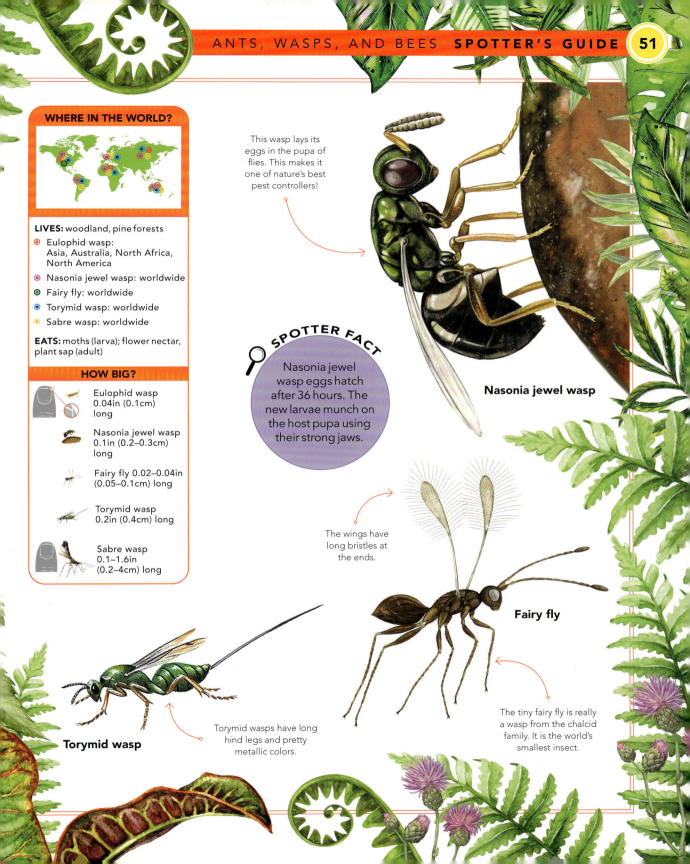

WHERE IN THE WORLD?

LIVES: woodland, pine forests
- Eulophid wasp: Asia, Australia, North Africa, North America
- Nasonia jewel wasp: worldwide
- Fairy fly: worldwide
- Torymid wasp: worldwide
- Sabre wasp: worldwide

EATS: moths (larva); flower nectar, plant sap (adult)

HOW BIG?

Eulophid wasp 0.04in (0.1cm) long

Nasonia jewel wasp 0.1in (0.2–0.3cm) long

Fairy fly 0.02–0.04in (0.05–0.1cm) long

Torymid wasp 0.2in (0.4cm) long

Sabre wasp 0.1–1.6in (0.2–4cm) long

This wasp lays its eggs in the pupa of flies. This makes it one of nature's best pest controllers!

Nasonia jewel wasp

SPOTTER FACT
Nasonia jewel wasp eggs hatch after 36 hours. The new larvae munch on the host pupa using their strong jaws.

The wings have long bristles at the ends.

Fairy fly

The tiny fairy fly is really a wasp from the chalcid family. It is the world's smallest insect.

Torymid wasp

Torymid wasps have long hind legs and pretty metallic colors.

ANTS, WASPS, AND BEES SPOTTER'S GUIDE 53

OAK GALL WASP

It's rare to spot the tiny oak gall wasp itself, but you may discover where it's been. Look for acorns with oddly shaped growths on them. These are called galls, and each contains one or more gall wasp larvae. You'll find brown galls on the ground, too. Inside each of those is a gall wasp pupa, waiting to emerge as an adult in spring.

WHERE IN THE WORLD?

LIVES: woodland, forests, parks, gardens, urban, worldwide
EATS: plant galls (larva); no food (adult)

HOW BIG?
up to 0.2in (0.5cm) long

Oak gall

The gall can grow to be nearly 1in (3cm) wide.

STRANGE KNOBBLES
Newly hatched larvae inject the tree with chemicals, which causes it to produce knobbly growths called galls. These surround the growing larvae, providing food and protection from predators.

DON'T MISS!
Different types of oak tree form galls with different shapes and colors. See how many types you can spot.

Gall wasp

Gall wasps are very small. Like many other wasps, they have a narrow waist.

IT'S WILD! Gall wasps are parasites. Their host is a plant rather than an animal.

54 SPOTTER'S GUIDE ANTS, WASPS, AND BEES

BEES

Bees are closely related to wasps and ants. These busy little creatures are excellent pollinators. They brush against flower pollen with their hairy bodies, and when they visit the next flower, they leave the pollen there. Some bees also make honey.

IN DANGER
The rusty-patched bumblebee is endangered. It is affected by disease, pesticides, and habitat loss.

Rusty-patched bumblebee

These bees are named after a patch of rust-red hair on the abdomens of the worker and male bees.

Western honeybee

Honeybees have long tongues so that they can reach the nectar in flowers. They live in hives.

ANTS, WASPS, AND BEES **SPOTTER'S GUIDE** 55

MAKING HONEY

Honey bees suck up nectar from flowers and turn it into honey. Bees store honey in lots of hexagon-shaped cells called honeycomb, which they make using wax from their bodies.

WHERE IN THE WORLD?

LIVES: grassland, woodland, marshland, sand dunes, parks, gardens

- Rusty-patched bumblebee: North America
- Western honeybee: worldwide
- Buff-tailed bumblebee: Europe
- Hairy-legged mining bee: Europe, Asia

EATS: flower pollen, flower nectar

STATUS:
- Rusty-patched bumblebee—critically endangered
- Hairy-legged mining bee—least concern

Buff-tailed bumblebee

The hairs on the bumblebee's body trap pollen from the flowers it visits. These bees live in nests in the ground or in wood.

HOW BIG?

 Rusty-patched bumblebee 0.4–0.6in (1–1.6cm) long

 Western honeybee 0.5–0.8in (1.3–2cm) long

 Buff-tailed bumblebee 0.4–0.8in (1–2cm) long

  Hairy-legged mining bee 0.5in (1.3cm) long

DON'T MISS!

Study the female mining bee. She has large, bright yellow pollen baskets on her hind legs and abdomen.

This mining bee uses its hairy legs to brush the sand away from its underground burrow.

Hairy-legged mining bee

BEETLES

SPOTTER'S GUIDE BEETLES

HOW TO SPOT BEETLES

Beetles belong to the order Coleoptera, the largest of all the insect groups. These bugs make up nearly half of all insects and a quarter of all known animal species. Look anywhere that leafy plants grow or rotting logs lie and you're almost certain to spot one.

BEETLE WATCH

Imagine exploring a rainforest, searching under fallen logs and under leaves for beetles. Notice them glinting in the sunlight with their metallic colors. Watch them as they scurry about searching for food.

LOOK LOW
Take a good look around and you'll probably spot a beetle. They often run across paths, so be careful as you walk.

Study the mouthparts
Beetles have biting or chewing mouthparts. In male giant stag beetles, these are elongated so that they look like huge pincers or horns.

Look at the body
All beetles have an exoskeleton, which includes hard cases to cover their wings.

Is it a predator?
Some beetles hunt for live insects to eat. Others, such as the stag beetle, feed on nectar, sap, and fruit.

Listen
Large beetles make a loud buzzing noise when they fly.

Giant stag beetle

BEETLES SPOTTER'S GUIDE 59

HOW DO BEETLES LIVE?

Beetles can both walk and fly. They rely on their hard bodies, warning colors, or camouflage to protect them from predators. Some look after their offspring, which is unusual in insects.

FRIEND OR FOE?

Some beetles cause damage to food crops. Others, such as the ladybug, eat the insects that harm many plants, making them useful to gardeners.

CLEVER MIMICS

Beetles can trick predators into thinking they are harmful. The long-horned beetle is safe to eat but has a red body and black spots, just like a toxic ladybug.

Long-horned beetle

Ladybug

CLEAN-UP GANG

Some species of beetle keep their habitat clean by getting rid of waste. Dung beetles bury elephant poop so that their larvae can eat it when they hatch.

WHAT MAKES A BEETLE?

Hard body: Beetles have a very hard body, called an exoskeleton.

Hard wing cases: A beetle's forewings are hardened into elytra, or wing cases. These protect the softer hindwings, which are used for flying.

Land and water: Beetles can be found in every habitat on land. Some are adapted to life in fresh water.

Males and females: Male beetles can look very different from the females. Sometimes they have large horns.

Warning colors: Bright colors and patterns warn predators that a beetle may be toxic or taste nasty.

Large copper dung beetle

60 SPOTTER'S GUIDE BEETLES

AMERICAN BURYING BEETLE

WHERE IN THE WORLD?

LIVES: soil, US
EATS: dead animals, insects, fly larvae
STATUS: ▬ critically endangered

HOW BIG?
1–1.9in (2.5–4.8cm) long

Meet the countryside's most efficient cleaners! Mated pairs of burying beetles find the dead bodies of birds and other small creatures and bury them—they are not left in the open to rot. These nocturnal flying beetles eat the bodies and use them as food for their offspring, too. The female lays her eggs near the buried carcass. As soon as they hatch, the larvae start munching until the whole body has disappeared.

The burying beetle has bright orange-red markings on its black body.

It can take up to eight hours for a pair of beetles to bury a dead animal.

Large, clublike antennae can detect a dead animal from a long way away.

American burying beetle

Both male and female parents take care of the larvae. This is unusual among insects.

IN DANGER
Scientists are not sure why this beetle is vanishing. They are breeding them in captivity to increase their numbers.

IT'S WILD! Several pairs of beetles often fight for a carcass among themselves until just the winning pair remains.

BEETLES **SPOTTER'S GUIDE** 61

VIOLIN BEETLE

Search on the ground to spot this violin-shaped beetle. Its flat body means it can hide in hollows or under bark.

WHERE IN THE WORLD?

LIVES: rainforests, Southeast Asia
EATS: other insects

HOW BIG?

 2.3–4in (6–10cm) long

The long antenna curve backward.

Part of the carapace, or hardened back, is see-through and feels like a leaf.

Violin beetle

ROVE BEETLE

Look for wild mushrooms if you want to see this beetle. It uses its huge mouthparts to chomp on the fungi.

WHERE IN THE WORLD?

LIVES: woodland, parks, Europe, Asia
EATS: other insects, fungi
STATUS: some species are near threatened to critically endangered

HOW BIG?

 0.3–0.8in (0.7–2cm) long

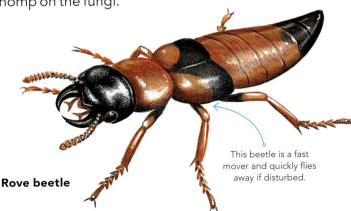

Rove beetle

This beetle is a fast mover and quickly flies away if disturbed.

SPOTTER'S GUIDE BEETLES

LARGE COPPER DUNG BEETLE

WHERE IN THE WORLD?

LIVES: grassland, forests, southern Africa
EATS: elephant dung

HOW BIG?

  1–1.2in (2.5–3cm) long

When you wander the southern African savanna in the summer months, take care not to step on the busy copper dung beetles. You'll see them everywhere, rolling small lumps of elephant dung into balls. The beetles bury the dung balls in the soft earth before the female lays a single egg inside each one. When the larvae hatch out, they eat the dung.

Large copper dung beetles are great for the environment, as they clean up smelly waste during the hot summer months.

The male uses his strong legs to push the ball to a special spot. Females often hitch a ride on top!

The black body has a copper-colored sheen.

The beetle has a strong sense of smell to find fresh dung.

Large copper dung beetle

A male and female sometimes work together to create a dung ball. This will be bigger than ones made by a single beetle.

BEETLES **SPOTTER'S GUIDE** 63

GIANT STAG BEETLE

WHERE IN THE WORLD?

LIVES: woodland, parks, gardens, US

EATS: rotten wood (larvae); rotting fruit, nectar, honeydew, tree sap (adults)

HOW BIG?

females 1.2–1.4in (3–3.5cm); males 1.7–2.3in (4.5–6cm) long

A flying giant stag beetle is a sight you won't forget. You'll hear the hum of its wings first. Then it lurches into view just above your head, looking like it could crash-land at any moment. Male beetles take to the air on warm summer evenings, seeking a mate. They use their huge jaws to fight off other males, just like stags, or male deer, use their antlers.

Giant stag beetles fly upright, holding their wings out behind them. It is usually the males that fly.

The male's jaws, or mandibles, look like the antlers of a stag. Females are smaller and don't have these large jaws.

The wings are tucked under elytra until the beetle needs to fly.

Giant stag beetle

SPOTTER FACT

If giant stag beetles flip over, they struggle to get upright again because of their heavy heads and flat backs.

IT'S WILD! Giant stag beetles can live for several years, mostly as larvae. They live as adults for only a few weeks.

64 SPOTTER'S GUIDE BEETLES

HERCULES BEETLE

WHERE IN THE WORLD?

LIVES: rainforests, Central and South America, Mexico, Caribbean
EATS: rotting fruit, tree sap

HOW BIG?

up to 7in (18cm) long

Explore the rainforest before dawn and you could see a jungle giant. The Hercules beetle is the longest in the world—about the length of an adult's hand! It's huge size is mainly due to the males' enormous horns, which are longer than the rest of its body. This beetle is also the world's largest flying bug.

SPOTTER FACT

This huge beetle is named after Hercules, the Greek hero. Hercules was known for his great strength.

Males have one horn on their head and another on their thorax. They use them for digging in the ground as well as fighting.

BATTLING MALES
Males fight each other for the right to mate with a female. They use their huge horns like a pair of pliers, lifting and squeezing their rival before tossing him to the ground.

BEETLES SPOTTER'S GUIDE 65

The Hercules beetle can carry things in its jaws that are many times heavier than its own body.

Adult beetles have an enormous appetite. They can eat for twenty-four hours without stopping.

The elytra are usually colored deep yellow to olive green.

Hercules beetle

The males' elytra change color depending on how wet it is. In very damp conditions, they become totally black.

DON'T MISS!

Listen for a huffing or hissing sound. That's the beetle rubbing its wings to scare off a predator.

SPOTTER'S GUIDE BEETLES

WHIRLIGIG BEETLE

WHERE IN THE WORLD?

LIVES: ponds, pools, worldwide
EATS: insects and other small creatures
STATUS: some species are endangered

HOW BIG?

 0.2–0.3in (0.5–0.7cm) long

Look on the surface of a pond to see groups of tiny whirligig beetles. They get their name from the way they swim around and around in circles.

The eyes are divided to allow the beetle to see above and below the water at the same time.

Whirligig beetle

FIRE-COLORED BEETLE

WHERE IN THE WORLD?

LIVES: woodland, forests, eastern US
EATS: honeydew, tree sap

HOW BIG?

0.3–0.7in (0.9–1.7cm) long

This bright orange beetle is easy to spot against green leaves. Lift the loose bark of rotting logs to see the flat-bodied, caterpillarlike larvae.

Males have large antennae that look like combs or antlers.

Fire-colored beetle

BEETLES **SPOTTER'S GUIDE** 67

GREAT DIVING BEETLE

This fast swimmer is a fierce hunter, attacking fish and frogs to eat. It traps air under its wing cases so it can stay underwater.

The bubble of air allows the beetle to breathe underwater while it waits for prey.

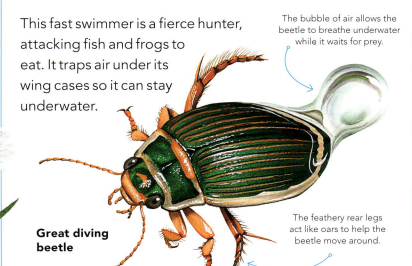

Great diving beetle

The feathery rear legs act like oars to help the beetle move around.

WHERE IN THE WORLD?

LIVES: weedy ponds and lakes, Europe
EATS: fish, tadpoles, dead creatures

HOW BIG?

1–1.4in (2.5–3.5cm) long

DARKLING BEETLE

This shiny black beetle lives in some of the driest places on Earth. It gets the water it needs when dew and ocean fog condense against its body.

Grooves direct the water toward the beetle's mouth.

Darkling beetle

WHERE IN THE WORLD?

LIVES: deserts, dry forests, worldwide
EATS: dead plants and animals, fungi
STATUS: 🍂 some species are critically endangered

HOW BIG?

up to 3in (7.5cm) long

68 SPOTTER'S GUIDE BEETLES

JEWEL BEETLE

This beetle's name is no surprise—just look at its beautiful, jewel-like colors! These beetles are easy to spot when the light catches their metallic sheen.

WHERE IN THE WORLD?

LIVES: woodland, parks, worldwide
EATS: leaves, nectar, pollen
STATUS: some species are endangered

HOW BIG?

up to 3in (8cm) long

The body can be long, round, or oval.

Jewel beetle

COLORADO BEETLE

WHERE IN THE WORLD?

LIVES: farms, gardens, North America, Europe
EATS: leaves, especially of potato plants

HOW BIG?

0.4in (1cm) long

The bright yellow, striped Colorado beetle loves to eat potato crops. It will happily eat tomato and eggplant plants as well.

The number of Colorado beetles can increase very quickly because they lay lots of eggs.

Colorado beetle

BEETLES **SPOTTER'S GUIDE** 69

FLEA BEETLE

You might see this little beetle jumping off a leaf. It has large hindlegs to help it leap around, but it can also walk and fly.

WHERE IN THE WORLD?

LIVES: fields, meadows, gardens, worldwide
EATS: plants

HOW BIG?

0.4in (1cm) long

Flea beetles are often dark and shiny, with metallic colors.

Flea beetle

PINE CHAFER

Listen in pine forests for the chunky pine chafer's loud screeching sounds. It makes these by rubbing its abdomen against its wing cases.

Splotchy white spots make the carapace look like marble.

Pine chafer

WHERE IN THE WORLD?

LIVES: pine forests, vineyards, central and southern Europe
EATS: pine needles

HOW BIG?

1.4–2in (3.5–5cm) long

The male has large, fan-like antennae.

SPOTTER'S GUIDE: BEETLES

WHERE IN THE WORLD?

LIVES: farmland, parks, gardens, worldwide
EATS: plants

HOW BIG?

up to 0.5in (1.2cm) long

TORTOISE BEETLE

Some members of this beetle family have a carapace that extends over their legs and head. This looks a bit like the flared edge of a tortoise's shell.

Tortoise beetles often have bright, metallic colors.

Tortoise beetle

WHERE IN THE WORLD?

LIVES: forests, Mexico, Central and South America
EATS: tree sap, wood, fungi

HOW BIG?

1.6–3in (4.3–7.5cm) long

HARLEQUIN BEETLE

Despite its bright red and yellow markings, this large beetle is surprisingly well-camouflaged on mossy tree trunks. You can spot it flying around at night.

The male's forelegs are longer than its whole body.

Harlequin beetle

BEETLES **SPOTTER'S GUIDE** 71

WHERE IN THE WORLD?

LIVES: grasslands, urban, Europe, northern Africa, introduced worldwide
EATS: dead animals, spiders, fruit, honeydew, human food

HOW BIG?
up to 6.5in (16.5cm) long

LONG-HORNED BEETLE

You'll know this beetle from its very long, curved antennae. Look for it on large flowers, trees, and dead wood.

Some species have warning colors and markings that make them look like ladybugs, ants, or wasps.

Long-horned beetle

BOMBARDIER BEETLE

A puff of smoke and a popping sound will alert you to the bombardier beetle. When threatened, it shoots a spray of boiling chemicals from its bottom.

The beetle can aim its toxic spray in any direction to ward off a predator.

Bombardier beetle

WHERE IN THE WORLD?

LIVES: grassland, woodland, worldwide
EATS: small insects

HOW BIG?
0.2–0.4in (0.5–1cm) long

SPOTTER'S GUIDE BEETLES

GOLIATH BEETLE

If you scan the trees and vines in Africa's rainforests, you'll spot one of the largest insects on the planet. The huge goliath beetle climbs up plants and trees to suck up sticky sap and munch on nutritious fruit. Named after the giant Goliath in the Bible, it's as big as an adult's palm and weighs as much as an apple.

WHERE IN THE WORLD?

LIVES: tropical rainforests, Africa
EATS: tree sap, ripe fruit, dung, wood, dead leaves

HOW BIG?

2–4in (5–10cm) long

SPOTTER FACT

The goliath beetle larva eats plants and rotting wood. It eventually weighs twice as much as the adult.

The wing cases can be plain reddish-brown or have brown, white, and black patterns.

The front part of the body is black with white stripes.

The male beetle's horns are at the front of the head and are shaped like a Y. He uses them to fight other males for food or mates.

The hooks on the beetle's legs help it to climb trees.

Goliath beetle

BEETLES **SPOTTER'S GUIDE** 73

AQUATIC FIREFLY

Despite its name, this little creature is not a fly at all—it's a beetle. Wander through rice paddies and around ponds at night and you could see the most beautiful twinkling light show. To attract a mate, male fireflies flash yellowish-green lights at the females from the end of their bodies. If the females are interested, they signal back with their own flashing lights.

WHERE IN THE WORLD?

LIVES: ponds, rice paddies, Taiwan, China
EATS: water snails (larva); nectar, pollen (adult)

HOW BIG?

0.3–0.4in (0.7–1.1cm) long

SPOTTER FACT

City lights are harmful to fireflies. They make it harder for the fireflies to see each other's flashing signals.

Fireflies taste bitter and are poisonous to some creatures. This is good protection from predators.

The firefly has an organ at the back of its body that makes light. It mixes oxygen from the air with chemicals inside its body to make it flash.

Aquatic firefly

IT'S WILD! Firefly larvae live underwater for about a year, feasting on water snails. The adults live for just two weeks and sometimes don't feed at all.

SPOTTER'S GUIDE BEETLES

WEEVILS

You'll know a weevil from other types of beetle because it has a long rostrum, or snout. Weevils love to munch on plants. Some species are considered pests because they can destroy whole fields of crops.

IN DANGER
The giraffe weevil lives only in the east of Madagascar. It is in danger because forests are being cut down.

These weevils are named after the giraffe because of the very long neck of the males.

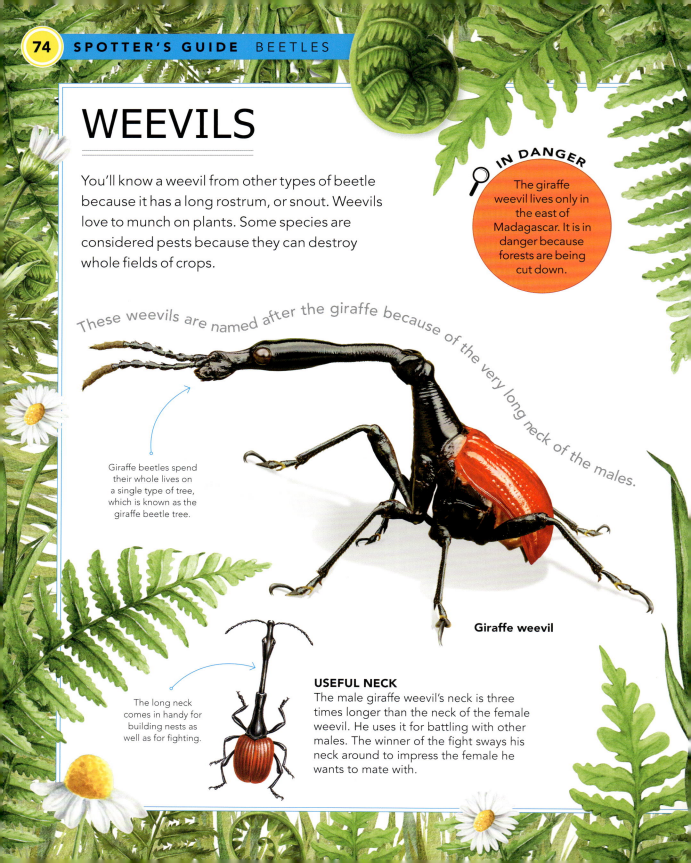

Giraffe beetles spend their whole lives on a single type of tree, which is known as the giraffe beetle tree.

Giraffe weevil

The long neck comes in handy for building nests as well as for fighting.

USEFUL NECK
The male giraffe weevil's neck is three times longer than the neck of the female weevil. He uses it for battling with other males. The winner of the fight sways his neck around to impress the female he wants to mate with.

BEETLES **SPOTTER'S GUIDE** 75

Two black stripes run down the length of the green body.

New Guinea weevil

SPOTTER FACT
Weevil larvae usually feed on just one part of a plant, such as the flower, stem, or roots.

Look on a plantain plant to find this tiny creature. It is this weevil's favorite food.

Plantain weevil

WHERE IN THE WORLD?

LIVES: rainforests, crop fields, grassland, scrubland
- Giraffe weevil: Madagascar
- New Guinea weevil: New Guinea
- Plantain weevil: Europe, North America

EATS: plants
STATUS: Giraffe weevil—near threatened

HOW BIG?
Giraffe weevil up to 1in (2.5cm) long

New Guinea weevil 0.9–1.3in (2.2–3.2cm) long

Plantain weevil up to 0.2in (0.6cm) long

SPOTTER'S GUIDE BEETLES

ORANGE LADYBUG

WHERE IN THE WORLD?

LIVES: woodland, parks, gardens, Europe, Asia
EATS: mildew

HOW BIG?
0.2in (0.6cm) long

Most ladybugs are red and black and love eating aphids, but this one is different. Its body is orange, and it has up to sixteen cream spots on its body. It is a plant eater, feeding on a white fungus called mildew. The orange ladybug is quite rare, but your best chance of spotting it is to look on sycamore and ash trees.

The edges of the elytra are semitransparent.

The female lays up to forty eggs at a time.

Orange ladybugs spend the winter hibernating under leaves and in wood crevices. They come out in summer.

Orange ladybug

LADYBUG LIFE CYCLE
Ladybugs lay their eggs in clutches. The larvae hatch after three to five days and spend two to three weeks eating. They shed their skin several times as they grow. Then each larva turns into a pupa. After seven to ten days, the adult ladybug emerges.

Larva

Pupa

Adult

IT'S WILD! When the adult emerges from the pupa, the colors on its soft body are pale. They deepen as the body hardens.

BEETLES **SPOTTER'S GUIDE** 77

CONVERGENT LADY BEETLE

This ladybug is common in North America, so you won't have any trouble finding one. It is an active predator, searching for small insects to eat as soon as it hatches from the egg. Lady beetles themselves are the favorite food of some other bugs, too, so they need to watch out!

WHERE IN THE WORLD?

LIVES: grassland, farmland, forests, parks, gardens, North America
EATS: aphids, scale insects, thrips

HOW BIG?

females 0.3in (0.8cm); males 0.2in (0.6cm) long

The two white strips look like they would converge, or meet, if they were longer. They give this ladybug its name.

The area behind the head is black with a white border.

Elytra are bright orange or red and usually have twelve black spots.

DON'T MISS!
Look out for large numbers of this ladybug. They gather together on plants to feed on soft-bodied insects.

Convergent lady beetle

SPOTTER'S GUIDE BEETLES

LADYBUGS

Look on any plant in spring and summer and you could find a ladybug scurrying around, searching for aphids to eat. These little beetles are easy to spot against green leaves because of their bright red, orange, or golden colors.

WHERE IN THE WORLD?

LIVES: grassland, forests, urban, close to rivers
- Five-spot: Europe
- Seven-spot: everywhere except Antarctica and the Arctic Circle
- Ten-spot: Europe, North Africa, western and eastern Asia

EATS: aphids, other insects

HOW BIG?

 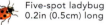
Five-spot ladybug 0.2in (0.5cm) long

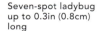
Seven-spot ladybug up to 0.3in (0.8cm) long

Ten-spot ladybug 0.2in (0.5cm) long

Ladybugs are often named after the number of spots they have.

Seven-spot ladybug

SPOTTER FACT

Ladybugs love to eat aphids. A single seven-spot ladybug can eat five thousand of them in its yearlong life.

The legs are usually black or dark gray.

BEETLES SPOTTER'S GUIDE 79

Five-spot ladybug

This species can be found on low plants near rivers.

This ladybug doesn't always have ten spots, but you can identify it by its brownish-orange legs.

Ten-spot ladybug

UP, UP, AND AWAY
When a ladybug is ready to fly, it opens its wing cases and unfolds its wings. The wing cases lift up and out to the side, while the wings beat quickly for takeoff.

ARACHNIDS

SPOTTER'S GUIDE ARACHNIDS

HOW TO SPOT ARACHNIDS

From the tiniest creature to one that's bigger than your hand, there are plenty of arachnids to find. Arachnids include spiders, scorpions, ticks, and mites. These bugs live in different places and may not, at first, look much like each other, but they all share similar features. How many types will you spot?

TREAD CAREFULLY
Spiders are very sensitive to vibrations and will quickly scuttle away if they sense you approaching. Move gently and quietly, taking care not to disturb them.

Count the legs
A spider's eight legs are arranged in four pairs.

ARACHNID WATCH
Imagine exploring a forest at night. Look down to spot spiders and scorpions scurrying along the ground or waiting in their burrows for passing prey. Look ahead to stop yourself from walking into a sticky spider's web.

Look at the body
The body is divided into the prosoma, which consists of the head and thorax, and the abdomen.

Study the behavior
Spiders, as well as many other arachnids, are predators. They lie in wait for prey to pass or to get caught in their silk webs.

Examine the mouth
Arachnids have mouthparts called pedipalps at the front of their heads. Some are so big that they look like another pair of legs.

Jumping spider

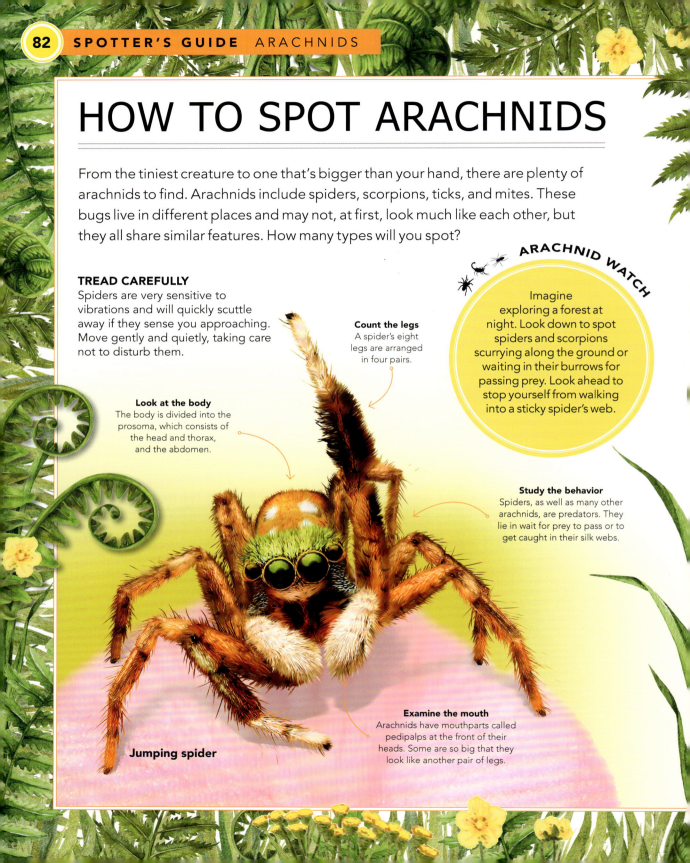

ARACHNIDS **SPOTTER'S GUIDE** 83

WHERE DO ARACHNIDS LIVE?
Arachnids can be found everywhere, from gardens, parks, forests, and deserts, to the corners of your home. They generally hide themselves away.

WHAT MAKES AN ARACHNID?

Body sections: Most arachnids have two body sections, unlike insects, which have three.

Number of legs: Arachnids have eight legs. These are attached to the front part of their body.

No wings or antennae: Arachnids can't fly and have no antennae like insects do.

Eyes: Arachnids have simple rather than compound eyes. Spiders usually have eight eyes positioned around their head.

GOOD DEFENDER
A deathstalker scorpion's pincers and sting are its greatest weapons. It uses them to fend off predators and catch its prey.

Deathstalker scorpion

GROWING BIGGER
Spiders grow by shedding their exoskeleton, or outer skin. They do this several times before they become adults.

TINY TICK
Ticks are some of the smallest arachnids. Many can't be seen with the naked eye. They are blood-sucking parasites that can transmit disease.

Dancing white lady

Sheep tick

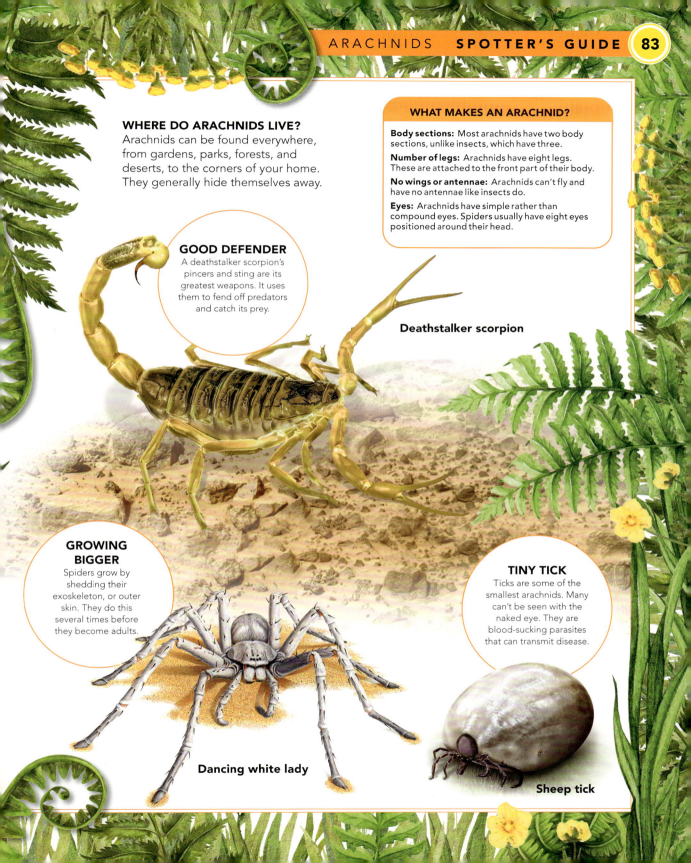

84 SPOTTER'S GUIDE ARACHNIDS

ORB WEAVERS

Orb weaver spiders get their name because they build orb-shaped, or spiral, webs. These can be more than 3 feet (1 m) wide, spanning the gaps between trees. If you accidentally walk into a web, the spider will quickly rebuild it. In fact, spiders prefer to have fresh, sticky webs every day to give themselves the best chance of catching prey.

Two very long, curved spines stick out from the female's hard, shiny abdomen. These can prevent predators from swallowing the spider.

Curved spiny spider

The golden orb spider is also known as the banana spider because of the shape of its long abdomen.

SPOTTER FACT

If its web is disturbed, a spider drops straight to the ground on an escape line. It returns when danger has passed.

There are many types of garden spider. This species has a large white cross of spots and streaks on its abdomen.

Golden orb spider

European garden spider

Male golden orb spiders are five to six times smaller than the females. They perch on the edge of her web when they are ready to mate.

The female has tufts of hair on her long legs.

ARACHNIDS **SPOTTER'S GUIDE** 85

SPINNING A WEB
An orb weaver starts by spinning a horizontal silk thread between two vertical supports, such as plant stems or tree trunks. Then it creates a frame of strong threads that look like spokes on a bicycle wheel. Lastly, the spider creates a thin spiral of silk, starting from the hub, or center. It can then sit on its hub and wait for prey to get stuck on the sticky threads.

WHERE IN THE WORLD?

LIVES: woodland, streams, grassland, wetland, gardens
- Long-jawed: Europe, Asia
- European garden: Europe, North America, Asia
- Marbled: North America, Europe, Asia
- Signature: South Asia
- Curved: South Asia
- Golden: North, Central, and South America, Caribbean, Australia, Africa, Asia

EATS: flies, wasps, other flying insects

STATUS:
- Long-jawed—vulnerable
- Golden—least concern

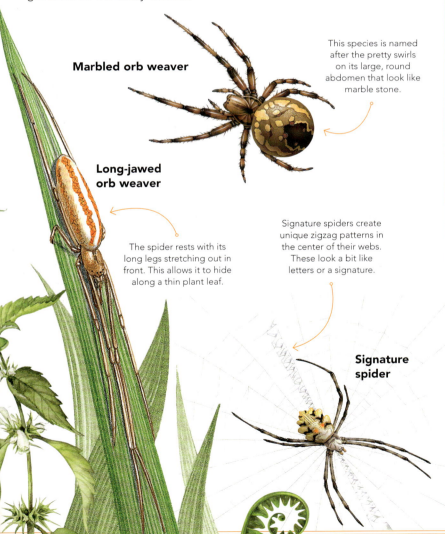

Marbled orb weaver

This species is named after the pretty swirls on its large, round abdomen that look like marble stone.

Long-jawed orb weaver

The spider rests with its long legs stretching out in front. This allows it to hide along a thin plant leaf.

Signature spiders create unique zigzag patterns in the center of their webs. These look a bit like letters or a signature.

Signature spider

HOW BIG?

 Long-jawed, females 0.5in (1.2cm); males 0.3in (0.9cm) long

 European garden, females 0.7in (1.8cm); males 0.3in (0.9cm) long

 Marbled, females 0.5in (1.4cm); males 0.3in (0.7cm) long

 Signature, females 0.5in (1.2 cm); males 0.2in (0.5 cm) long

 Curved, females 0.4in (1cm) without horns; males 0.2in (0.5cm) long

 Golden, females 0.9–1.6in (2.4–4cm) long; males 0.2in (0.6cm) long

SPOTTER'S GUIDE ARACHNIDS

FUNNEL WEB SPIDER

WHERE IN THE WORLD?

LIVES: damp, rocky forests; logs; gardens; Australia
EATS: insects, snails, small mammals, reptiles, birds, bats, frogs

HOW BIG?
females 1.5in (3.8cm); males 1in (2.5cm) long

In the damp forests of Australia lives one of the country's most feared spiders—the funnel web. Not all members of this family are harmful, but several are known for their very powerful venom. These creatures don't bite unless provoked, so take care not to disturb their burrows. You'll spot these because of the delicate silk triplines that fan out in a funnel shape from the entrance.

VENOMOUS FANGS
A spider's venom is stored inside the fangs. When the spider bites, the venom is released into its victim.

After it has bitten, the long fangs often get stuck in the skin. The spider has to be flicked off.

There is no obvious body pattern.

This part of the body is called the carapace. In funnel web spiders, it is always shiny.

Two of the four spinnerets, or spinning organs, stick out at the back.

Funnel web spider

IT'S WILD! When a creature touches the funnel web's silk triplines, the spider leaps out of its burrow to grab it.

ARACHNIDS SPOTTER'S GUIDE 87

TARANTULA

WHERE IN THE WORLD?

LIVES: tropical forests, dry regions, worldwide

EATS: centipedes, millipedes, other spiders, frogs, mice, small birds

HOW BIG?

2–4.3in (5–11cm) long

Look down to your feet as well as above your head if you want to find a tarantula. These large, slow-moving spiders can live in underground burrows or in trees.

A tarantula bite is painful but harmless. The mild venom is less toxic than a bee sting.

Tarantula

TRAPDOOR SPIDER

This timid spider spends most of its life hiding underground in its tube-shaped burrow. It covers the entrance with a trapdoor made of soil, leaves, and silk and lies in wait for passing prey.

The trapdoor spider's eight eyes are arranged in two rows of four.

The abdomen ends in a circular shield that is the exact width of its burrow. It can use it to seal itself in if threatened.

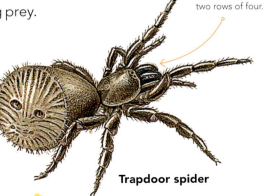

Trapdoor spider

WHERE IN THE WORLD?

LIVES: underground burrows in damp, shaded slopes; North America; Southeast Asia

EATS: crickets, grasshoppers, moths, beetles

HOW BIG?

females 1.2in (3cm); males 0.7in (1.9cm) long

88 SPOTTER'S GUIDE ARACHNIDS

JUMPING SPIDER

WHERE IN THE WORLD?

LIVES: tropical forests, Central America
EATS: acacia leaf buds, nectar, flies, ant larvae

HOW BIG?
0.2in (0.5–0.6cm) long

In the acacia trees of Central America lives an unusual and cunning spider. It's mostly vegetarian—nearly all other spiders are meat eaters—and it loves to eat tasty acacia leaf buds. This tiny jumping spider shares its home with ferocious ants, which work all day breaking off leaf buds to eat. When the coast is clear, the spider jumps in to steal some of the juicy buds for its own dinner.

DANCE ROUTINE
Male jumping spiders do a special dance to attract females. This involves showing off their hairy legs by raising and lowering them in different ways. The males also slide sideways or zigzag, and buzz like a drum roll.

Two of the spider's eight eyes are much bigger than the others. Scientists think jumping spiders can see more colors than humans can.

Jumping spider

The male's legs are covered with amber-colored hairs. The female's legs are lighter yellow.

IT'S WILD! This spider can jump nearly fifty times its own body length using its powerful back legs.

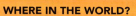

ARACHNIDS **SPOTTER'S GUIDE** 89

SPITTING SPIDER

WHERE IN THE WORLD?

LIVES: under stones, caves, buildings, worldwide
EATS: moths, flies, silverfish

HOW BIG?

up to 0.2in (0.6cm) long

This long-legged spider wanders around slowly at night. Watch it catch its prey from a distance by squirting it with a sticky mixture of silk and venom.

The dome-shaped body is light brown with black spots.

Spitting spider

The venomous goo pins its prey to the ground.

VIOLIN SPIDER

WHERE IN THE WORLD?

LIVES: under stones and loose bark, caves, buildings, southern Europe, North Africa
EATS: small insects

HOW BIG?

up to 0.3in (0.8cm) long

If you've ever wondered how this spider gets its name, see the dark mark on its carapace, which looks like a violin. You can find it roaming around at night, looking to catch its next meal.

Violin spider

The dark marking is the shape of a violin.

SPOTTER'S GUIDE ARACHNIDS

WIDOW SPIDERS

Widow spiders are some of the most venomous in the world. Don't worry—they are very timid and quickly run away if you disturb their tangly webs. The female is much bigger than the male, and she sometimes eats him after mating. This is what gives widow spiders their name.

Southern black widow

The female hangs upside down in her web, waiting for her prey.

SPOTTER FACT

The females lay up to 750 eggs. Only about twelve of her babies reach adulthood.

Females have a red hourglass shape on the underside of their abdomen.

These widows have striped legs.

Brown widow

ARACHNIDS **SPOTTER'S GUIDE** 91

Northern black widow

The northern black widow has a line of red spots on its abdomen.

The red widow has orange-red spots on its abdomen and bright red legs.

Red widow

Redback

This Australian spider is closely related to America's western black widow.

WHERE IN THE WORLD?

LIVES: rotten wood, rock piles, buildings
- Southern black widow: North America
- Northern black widow: North America
- Brown widow: Africa, but found worldwide
- Red widow: North America
- Redback: Australia, New Zealand

EATS: flies, crickets, moths, beetles, woodlice, other spiders, small lizards

HOW BIG?

 Southern black widow, females 1.5in (3.8cm); males 0.5in (1.2cm) long

 Northern black widow, females 1.5in (3.8cm); males 0.2in (0.6cm) long

 Brown widow, females 0.5in (1.3cm); males 0.3in (0.7cm) long

 Red widow, females 1.5–2in (3.8–5cm); males 0.5in (1.2cm) long

 Redback, females 0.5in (1.4cm); males 0.2in (0.4cm) long

IT'S WILD! Male black widow spiders are brown or gray with little red spots. They are hardly ever seen by people.

SPOTTER'S GUIDE   ARACHNIDS

HOUSE SPIDER

Chances are you'll find this spider somewhere in your house. It likes to hide in dark corners where it can build large webs.

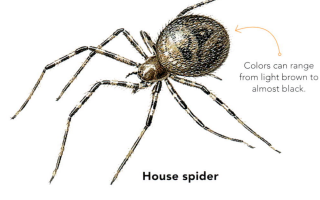

Colors can range from light brown to almost black.

House spider

WHERE IN THE WORLD?

LIVES: buildings, woodland, scrubland, parks, gardens, worldwide

EATS: insects

HOW BIG?

 0.2in (0.4–0.6cm) long

WOLF SPIDER

WHERE IN THE WORLD?

LIVES: grassland, heathland and moorland, woodland, wetland, parks, gardens, worldwide

EATS: insects, cockroaches

HOW BIG?

 0.2–1in (0.6–2.5cm) long

Look on the ground for this fearsome predator. Using its excellent eyesight, it captures its prey by pouncing on it, just like a wolf.

The mother carries her spiderlings, or baby spiders, on her back for several weeks.

Wolf spider

IT'S WILD! When they are old enough, spiderlings use silk "parachutes" to float away on the breeze.

ARACHNIDS **SPOTTER'S GUIDE** 93

DAVID BOWIE HUNTSMAN SPIDER

This large hunting spider is named after the famous musician David Bowie, who had an orange-haired alter ego named Ziggy Stardust. This speedy, orange spider might look like him, but it's quite shy—not like a pop star at all!

WHERE IN THE WORLD?

LIVES: tropical forests, Southeast Asia
EATS: insects, other spiders

HOW BIG?

 females 1in (2.5cm); males 0.6in (1.5cm) long

The hairs on its legs sense the vibrations of animals moving around on the ground.

These spiders hunt and chase down their prey rather than trap them in webs.

David Bowie huntsman spider

Its long legs help this spider to run fast.

SPOTTER FACT
The David Bowie huntsman hides in dark places during the day. It comes out to hunt at night.

HUNTSMAN SPIDER LIFE CYCLE
The female huntsman makes a flat, oval egg sac from silk and lays up to two hundred eggs inside. After three weeks, the spiderlings hatch out. The young spiders are pale and molt several times, shedding their exoskeleton so that they can grow. Adult huntsman have harder bodies and are darker brown.

Egg sac and eggs | **Spiderling** | **Young spider** | **Adult spider**

SPOTTER'S GUIDE ARACHNIDS

DANCING WHITE LADY

WHERE IN THE WORLD?

LIVES: deserts, Namibia
EATS: insects, other spiders, lizards

HOW BIG?

up to 1.3in (3.2cm) long

This large spider spends the day hidden in burrows made of silk and sand to escape the hot sun. Look for it in the cool night as it lies in wait for prey.

The legspan can be 4–5.5in (10–14cm).

Dancing white lady

The spider sends messages to other white ladies by drumming its legs on the ground.

BRAZILIAN WANDERING SPIDER

Watch your step as you creep through the forest at night. This large spider is one of the most venomous in the world, and it's not afraid to bite you if you cross its path.

Brazilian wandering spider

Strong legs help make this a fast and agile spider.

WHERE IN THE WORLD?

LIVES: forests, banana plantations, wasteland, buildings, South America
EATS: large insects, small invertebrates

HOW BIG?

females 1.4–2in (3.5–5cm); males 1in (2.5cm) long

ARACHNIDS **SPOTTER'S GUIDE** 95

RAFT SPIDER

This spider doesn't need a raft or any sort of boat to cross the water, despite its name. Its long legs spread its weight across the water's surface, which stops it from sinking. You'll find it waiting patiently at the water's edge. As soon as the spider feels a movement in the water, it quickly runs across the surface or dives underneath to catch its prey.

WHERE IN THE WORLD?

LIVES: wetland, lakes, ponds, marshes, Europe, West Asia
EATS: insects, small fish, tadpoles

HOW BIG?

females 0.9in (2.2cm);
males 0.6in (1.5cm) long

IN DANGER

The raft spider is very rare. Many of its watery habitats have become polluted or been lost.

The raft spider can hide underwater for up to an hour, breathing air from bubbles trapped in its body hair.

Cream or white bands run down each side of the body.

The back legs usually hold on to water plants as it sits waiting.

Raft spider

The front legs rest on the water so that it can feel for vibrations made by passing prey.

The male spider taps his legs on the water's surface to attract a female to mate with.

IT'S WILD! The raft spider lays its eggs in a special nursery web that it guards until the spiderlings hatch.

SPOTTER'S GUIDE ARACHNIDS

MOUSE SPIDER

WHERE IN THE WORLD?

LIVES: forests, shrubland, Australia
EATS: insects, other spiders, frogs, lizards

HOW BIG?

females 1.4in (3.5cm); males 0.6in (1.5cm) long

You're unlikely to spot a female mouse spider, as she rarely leaves her trapdoor-covered burrow, but look for the male as he scuttles about.

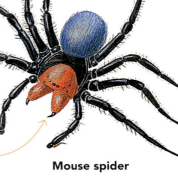

The male has bright red jaws and a large, shiny head.

Mouse spider

HEATHER SPIDER

WHERE IN THE WORLD?

LIVES: heathland, meadows, Europe, North Africa, Asia
EATS: insects

HOW BIG?

females 0.3–0.4in (0.7–1.1cm); males 0.2in (0.4cm) long

This pretty pink creature is a type of crab spider. These spiders get their name from their crab-shaped bodies and the way they move sideways or backward like a crab.

The heather spider is well-camouflaged against purplish heather plants.

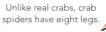

Heather spider

Unlike real crabs, crab spiders have eight legs.

ARACHNIDS **SPOTTER'S GUIDE** 97

FLOWER CRAB SPIDER

You would have to wait for days to see the cunning flower crab spider perform her special trick. Very, very slowly, the female changes color to match the flower she is resting on. She lies in wait there for passing insects. The spider is so well camouflaged that her prey—and you—have to look hard to spot her.

WHERE IN THE WORLD?

LIVES: meadows, woodland, grassland, scrubland, gardens, Europe, North America, West Asia
EATS: insects, flower pollen

HOW BIG?

females 0.4in (1cm); males 0.2in (0.5cm) long

Female spiders can be yellow or white, depending on the type of flower they are hiding on. It can take up to twenty days for them to change color.

Flower crab spiders hold their legs to the sides.

Long, strong legs mean the spider can catch prey much bigger than itself.

Flower crab spider

CRAB SPIDER HEAD
A crab spider's eight small eyes are widely spaced. Two bulbous fangs deliver a powerful venom to paralyze insects.

SPOTTER FACT

Females balance on bare stems and stretch their legs out to make themselves look like a flower.

SPOTTER'S GUIDE ARACHNIDS

SHEEP TICK

A tick is a parasite, which means it lives and feeds on a host, or another animal. Sheep ticks don't just live on sheep. You can also find these tiny creatures on large mammals such as horses, cows, deer, dogs—and humans! If you see one that is swollen, it's because it's just had a huge meal of blood.

WHERE IN THE WORLD?

LIVES: on large mammals, Europe, North Africa
EATS: blood

HOW BIG?
0.1in (0.2–0.3cm) long

The sheep tick's body is plain and smooth.

Ticks are normally flat. They can swell up to three or four times their normal size after feeding.

Sheep ticks live on three different animals during their lifetime. The larvae prefer small insect eaters such as hedgehogs and moles.

SPOTTER FACT
Sheep ticks don't have eyes. A body part called a Haller's organ helps them sense their surroundings by smell.

Sheep tick

There are two long palps at the front of the head.

IT'S WILD! Sheep ticks carry many diseases that are dangerous to people as well as animals.

ARACHNIDS SPOTTER'S GUIDE 99

DEATHSTALKER SCORPION

This arachnid has a mighty sting in its tail. Scorpions look a bit like small lobsters, with a pair of pincers and a thin tail that curls over their back. Beware the poisonous tip, called a telson. It can deliver a powerful venom that stuns or kills predators and prey much larger than itself.

WHERE IN THE WORLD?

LIVES: deserts, North Africa, Middle East
EATS: insects, spiders, worms

HOW BIG?
3–4.2in (7.6–10.8cm) long

SPOTTER FACT
Scorpions are super survivors. They can cope with extreme heat and cold and live off just one insect per year.

The deathstalker has one of the most powerful venoms of any scorpion. It can kill predators such as lizards, birds, and snakes.

If the deathstalker scorpion can't find any other food, it will eat another deathstalker. This is called cannibalism.

Scorpions grab prey with their pincers before stinging them with their tails.

DON'T MISS!
Scorpions hide during the day. Watch them at night to see them in battle with their prey.

Deathstalker scorpion

IT'S WILD! Scorpions existed before the dinosaurs. Fossils show they haven't changed much in millions of years.

SPOTTER'S GUIDE: ARACHNIDS

PSEUDOSCORPION

WHERE IN THE WORLD?

LIVES: leaf litter in woodland and grassland, sand dunes, buildings, worldwide
EATS: dead animals, insects, fly larvae
STATUS: some species are critically endangered

HOW BIG?

0.1–0.3in (0.2–0.8cm) long

With its large pincers, this tiny bug resembles a scorpion, but really, it is a different species. It is called a pseudoscorpion because it is like a scorpion—*pseudo* means "false" in Greek. If you look closely, you can see that it doesn't have a scorpion's curly tail and stinger.

IN DANGER
Some peudoscorpions are threatened. One species is found only in one cave on one island in the Atlantic Ocean.

The body is shaped like a pear.

Pseudoscorpions often hitch a ride with a larger creature to get to new places.

These tiny creatures eat many common household pests, such as dust mites, book lice, and the larvae of clothes moths.

After paralyzing its prey with its venomous pincers, a pseudoscorpion uses its digestive juices to dissolve it down so that it can suck up its remains.

Pseudoscorpion

ARACHNIDS SPOTTER'S GUIDE   101

SUN SPIDER

WHERE IN THE WORLD?

LIVES: warm, dry leaf litter or under stones in forests; scrubland and grassland; North, Central, and South America; Africa; Europe; Asia

EATS: termites, beetles, snakes, small lizards, birds, rodents

HOW BIG?

 up to 2.7in (7cm) long

This arachnid has many names, such as camel spider, wind scorpion, and jerrymander. It is aggressive by nature, with a powerful bite, but is harmless to humans.

Sun spider

On the last pair of legs are two racquet organs. These help the sun spider to detect threats, mates, and prey.

HARVESTMAN

Harvestmen get their name because they are found in great numbers at harvest time. They have a small, round body and very long, spindly legs.

WHERE IN THE WORLD?

LIVES: woodland, fields, gardens, buildings, worldwide

EATS: insects, bird droppings, fruit, fungi

HOW BIG?

0.3in (0.8cm) long

Harvestman

The legs have hooks on the ends to catch small insects.

SPOTTER'S GUIDE — ARACHNIDS

MITES

One of the tiniest types of arachnid is the mite. You may struggle to see one, but they are everywhere—on plants, in water, in the earth, and on humans and other animals. Most are harmless, but some create allergies and spread disease.

WHERE IN THE WORLD?

LIVES:
- Varroa mite: on bees, in beehives, worldwide
- Oribatid mite: soil, worldwide
- Red velvet mite: soil, leaf litter, worldwide

EATS: honeybee body tissue, fungus, bacteria, termites, spiders, beetles

HOW BIG?

- Varroa mite 0.1in (0.2cm) long
- Oribatid mite 0.1in (0.2cm) long
- Red velvet mite up to 0.2in (0.4cm) long

The body is covered in lots of tiny red hairs, which look like velvet.

This parasite lives on other arthropods.

Red velvet mite

ARACHNIDS **SPOTTER'S GUIDE** 103

The hard, shiny cuticle is waterproof. It stops the mite's body from becoming waterlogged or drying out.

SPOTTER FACT
Oribatid mites make healthy soil. They eat harmful fungus and bacteria and replace vital nutrients as they poop.

Each leg ends in a claw, with tiny hairs that help the mite grip the soil as it moves.

Oribatid mite

SPOTTER FACT
Varroa mites mate inside beehives. Only the females leave the hive, hitching a ride on an adult bee.

Its flat shape helps the female to lodge itself between a bee's body segments. It then feeds on its soft tissue.

This mite is a parasite. It lives on honey bees and in beehives.

Varroa mite

TRUE FLIES

SPOTTER'S GUIDE TRUE FLIES

HOW TO SPOT TRUE FLIES

Lots of insects can fly, but the ones known as true flies have just one pair of wings—all other flying insects have two pairs. The scientific name for true flies is Diptera. This group includes blood-sucking mosquitos and expert assassins like the robber fly. True flies are found nearly everywhere on the planet, both indoors and out, so you're sure to spot one.

LOOK UP
True flies are amazing in the air. See them zipping around above your head.

Study the antennae
The robber fly's short antennae stick out horizontally from its head. The antennae of other true flies can be long and thin or feathery.

Examine the eyes
True flies have both simple and compound eyes. The robber fly's compound eyes allow it to see what's around it.

Look at the body
To help them fly speedily, true flies have short, streamlined bodies.

Gripping feet
True flies have special claws or pads on their feet to help them grip onto surfaces.

Robber fly

TRUE FLIES **SPOTTER'S GUIDE** 107

HOW DO FLIES LIVE?
Adult true flies have a fairly short lifespan—about fifteen to thirty days. Some, such as the pine needle midge, live for just two or three days.

Black soldier fly

VARIED DIET
True flies can be plant eaters, insect hunters, parasites, or scavengers. The black soldier fly larva performs a valuable service by eating up plant and animal waste.

TRUE FLY WATCH
Imagine watching a true fly in the air. Note where it lands and how long it stays there. Look at how differently the members of this group fly. Some zoom, while others hover in one place or loop around lazily.

CLEVER LOOK-ALIKES
True flies can be good mimics. Although harmless, the hover fly has markings like a wasp or bee, which animals avoid because of their sting.

Hover fly

SUPER SUCKERS
Some true flies suck up fruit juices and sap. Others, like the tiger mosquito, have piercing mouths for drinking blood.

Tiger mosquito

WHAT MAKES A TRUE FLY?

Two wings: True flies have a single pair of wings.

Balancing organs: Instead of hindwings, true flies have two drumstick-shaped organs called halteres. These help them balance in flight.

Feeding: All true flies are liquid feeders. To break up solid food, they use their saliva, or spit, to soften it before sucking it up.

Legless larvae: True fly larvae are called maggots. They have no jointed legs.

SPOTTER'S GUIDE: TRUE FLIES

STALK-EYED FLY

WHERE IN THE WORLD?

LIVES: warm and wet areas, Southeast Asia, southern Africa, North America, Europe
EATS: dead plants and animals

HOW BIG?
0.2–0.5in (0.4–1.2cm) long

As you creep through a tropical jungle at night, look down at low-growing plants near water to see a group of very strange-looking creatures. The stalk-eyed fly's head has long stalks on either side that each end in an eye. Scientists aren't sure why the fly has evolved this way, but they do know that the female chooses the male with the longest eye stalks as her mate.

At night, the flies roost in small groups on leaves or threadlike root hairs hanging near water. They return to the same site each day.

DON'T MISS! Watch out for males trying to knock each other over. The winner takes control of the roosting site.

These flies feed on fungi and bacteria from decaying plants.

Stalk-eyed fly

SPOTTER FACT Stalk-eyed flies have existed for about 50 million years. Scientists know this from the fossils they have found.

Eye stalks are up to 0.4in (1cm) long. The distance between the eyes can be greater than the body length.

The antennae are also located on the eye stalks. All other flies have antennae in the middle of their head.

IT'S WILD! As soon as it has hatched, the fly pumps air to the tips of the eye stalks to stretch them out while they are still soft.

TRUE FLIES **SPOTTER'S GUIDE** 109

CRANE FLY

If you see something huge and spindly, it's probably a crane fly. These gangly insects are often called daddy longlegs because of their long limbs.

WHERE IN THE WORLD?

LIVES: cool, moist areas near water; worldwide
EATS: no food or some flower nectar and pollen
STATUS: least concern

HOW BIG?

0.3–1.4in (0.7–3.5cm) long

The legspan of a crane fly can be 4in (10cm).

There are more than 15,000 types of crane fly. All are completely harmless.

Crane fly

SAND FLY

You'll recognize the sand fly by its weak, hopping flight. It thrives in warm, damp climates, but it can live anywhere—even in your home.

The sand fly holds its hairy wings vertically in a V shape when it is resting.

The female feeds on blood. The bite can leave a nasty rash.

Sand fly

WHERE IN THE WORLD?

LIVES: sandy soil, Central and South America, southern Europe, Africa, Asia
EATS: blood (female); nectar, honeydew (males and females)

HOW BIG?

0.1in (0.2–0.3cm) long

SPOTTER'S GUIDE | TRUE FLIES

DROSOPHILA FRUIT FLY

Look at your fruit bowl on a warm day and you could see a little brown creature dozily flying around. The drosophila fruit fly is attracted to the sugary juices of ripe fruit.

Tiny bristles help the fly sense movement nearby.

Drosophila fruit fly

WHERE IN THE WORLD?

LIVES: near fruit and rotting food, worldwide
EATS: fruit, rotting food

HOW BIG?

0.1–0.2in (0.2–0.4cm) long

TEPHRITID FRUIT FLY

This colorful fruit fly lays its eggs in fruit and vegetables. After they hatch, the larvae munch their way through the plants to store up energy for becoming a pupa.

Some species of tephritids feed on only one type of fruit or vegetable.

Tephritid fruit fly

WHERE IN THE WORLD?

LIVES: orchards, farmland, worldwide
EATS: fruit, vegetables, plants (larva); pollen, flower nectar, honeydew (adult)

HOW BIG?

0.1–0.4in (0.2–1cm) long

DON'T MISS! Watch out for interesting wing movements from these flies. They do them as part of courtship or to guard territory.

TRUE FLIES **SPOTTER'S GUIDE** 111

BLACK SOLDIER FLY

Many insects are pests to humans, but the black soldier fly is a superhero. Its larvae are huge eaters. They gobble up household food scraps and farm waste and recycle them through their poop. This can then be used as nutritious compost and animal feed. There's less waste for people to get rid of and more goodness returned to the soil.

WHERE IN THE WORLD?

LIVES: farmland, gardens, worldwide
EATS: plant and animal waste (larva); flower nectar (adult)

HOW BIG?

0.1in (0.2cm) long

SPOTTER FACT
Black soldier fly larvae can themselves be fed to animals. This saves farmers having to grow or buy crops for feed.

The black soldier fly has a wide head.

The body is black with blue-green metallic colors.

The hind legs are pale.

Black soldier fly

IT'S WILD! The adult flies hardly eat at all. They don't fly around much, as they have very little energy.

SPOTTER'S GUIDE **TRUE FLIES**

DEER FLY

In late spring and summer, the female deer fly feasts on animal and human blood, which she needs in order to produce eggs. She can give a painful bite!

Deer fly

Many deer flies have very colorful compound eyes.

Big wings shaped like fans help them fly quickly over long distances.

WHERE IN THE WORLD?

LIVES: woodland, wetlands, worldwide
EATS: pollen (male); blood (female)

HOW BIG?

0.2–0.3in (0.5–0.7cm) long

HORSE FLY

Female horse flies are bloodsuckers. They use two powerful blades in their mouth to slice open the flesh of animals so they can drink their blood.

Some horseflies have bands of color across their eyes.

The body is quite stocky.

Horse fly

SPOTTER FACT

The eyes of the male horse flies meet at the front of the head. The females' eyes are separated.

WHERE IN THE WORLD?

LIVES: woodland, wetlands, marshes, worldwide
EATS: flower nectar, honeydew, plant sap (male); blood (female)

HOW BIG?

0.5–1.2in (1.2–3cm) long

TRUE FLIES **SPOTTER'S GUIDE** 113

HOUSE FLY

WHERE IN THE WORLD?

LIVES: buildings, worldwide
EATS: human food, feces (poop)

HOW BIG?

0.2–0.3in (0.6–0.7cm) long

What's that buzzing noise? It's a house fly flying around your house, looking for something to eat. Cover your food or you could find it sharing your meal!

The house fly's compound eyes are bright red.

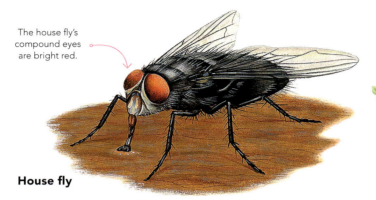

House fly

HOVER FLY

Hover flies have an amazing skill—they can stay in one spot in the air. They are a gardener's friend, as the larvae eat aphids, a major pest to plants.

WHERE IN THE WORLD?

LIVES: gardens, farmland, near water, worldwide
EATS: flower nectar, pollen, aphids

HOW BIG?

0.1–1in (0.3–2.5cm) long

Some hover flies look like wasps or bees—but they have one pair of wings, not two.

Hover fly

SPOTTER'S GUIDE TRUE FLIES

MOSQUITOS

Mosquitos are found in warm, damp climates. If you're camping out and hear a faint whining sound—beware! It's likely to be a mosquito flying around, preparing to suck your blood. They leave an itchy bump where they've bitten.

Culex mosquitos are brownish all over without any pattern.

Culex mosquito

This mosquito gets its name from the stripes on its body and legs.

Tiger mosquito

SPOTTER FACT

Mosquitos are said to be the world's most dangerous animal because of the serious diseases they transmit.

TRUE FLIES **SPOTTER'S GUIDE** 115

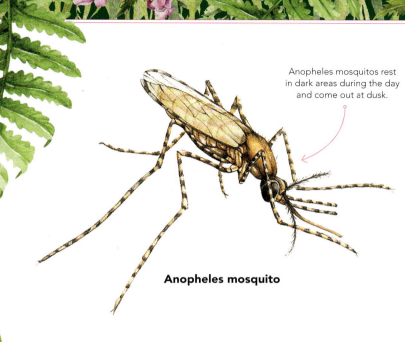

Anopheles mosquitos rest in dark areas during the day and come out at dusk.

Anopheles mosquito

WHERE IN THE WORLD?

LIVES: forests, urban, countryside

- Tiger mosquito: Southeast Asia, North, Central, and South America, Europe
- Anopheles mosquito: Asia, Africa, North, Central, and South America, Europe
- Culex mosquito: worldwide

EATS: blood (female); plant juices, flower nectar (female and male)

HOW BIG?

Tiger mosquito 0.1–0.4in (0.2–1cm) long

Anopheles mosquito 0.2in (0.5cm) long

 Culex mosquito 0.2–0.4in (0.4–1cm) long

MOSQUITO LIFE CYCLE
Female mosquitos lay their eggs in fresh water. Depending on the species, eggs can be laid singly or stuck together to form a raft. After hatching, the larvae feed on algae and bacteria in the water until they are ready to turn into a pupa. When they emerge as adult mosquitos, they fly away.

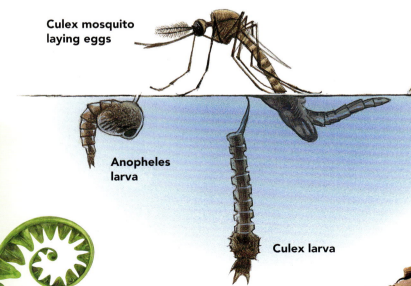

Culex mosquito laying eggs

Egg raft

Anopheles larva

Culex larva

116 | **SPOTTER'S GUIDE** — TRUE FLIES

GREEN BOTTLE FLY

It's very common to see this fly in spring when it emerges from hibernation. You'll recognize it by the bright green metallic sheen on its body.

The green bottle fly has short black bristles and three grooves across its thorax.

WHERE IN THE WORLD?

LIVES: warm and moist areas, coasts, worldwide
EATS: dead animals, feces (poop), pollen, flower nectar

HOW BIG?

0.4–0.5in (1–1.4cm) long

Green bottle fly

MIDGE

WHERE IN THE WORLD?

LIVES: ponds, lakes, worldwide
EATS: flower nectar, tree sap (male); blood (female)

HOW BIG?

less than 0.1in (0.1cm) long

These tiny insects love warm, damp weather. They come out at dawn and dusk—but only if it's still. They aren't strong enough to fly in the wind.

The body is slender, like a mosquito's.

The male's antennae are feathery.

Midge

TRUE FLIES **SPOTTER'S GUIDE** 117

NEEDLE MIDGE

The needle midge gets its name because its larvae burrow into pine needles to grow. You'll find them in Douglas fir forests. These tiny, delicate orange flies are hard to spot with the naked eye. Instead, you might see lots of purplish pine needles on the ground, some with a gall, or swelling, underneath. These show that the larvae have eaten the needles from the inside and hatched out.

WHERE IN THE WORLD?

LIVES: Douglas fir tree forests, North America, western Europe
EATS: Douglas fir pine needles (larva); no food (adult)

HOW BIG?

0.1in (0.3cm) long

SPOTTER FACT
Needle midges can cause serious damage to Douglas firs. These are used as Christmas trees in some countries.

Adult needle midges live for two to four days. In this very short time, they have to find a mate and the females have to lay eggs.

The female lays her eggs through a long tube at the back of her body called an ovipositor.

SPOTTER'S GUIDE TRUE FLIES

ROBBER FLY

WHERE IN THE WORLD?

LIVES: grassy fields near woodland, North America

EATS: other insect larvae, worms (larva); small flying insects (adult)

HOW BIG?

0.5–0.7cm (0.2–0.3in) long

Powerful and bristly, the robber fly is a flying ace. When another flying insect passes, the robber fly quickly takes off from its resting place. It skillfully grabs the insect in midair and injects it with its poisonous saliva—all in two blinks of an eye. No wonder it's sometimes called the assassin fly!

As well as two large compound eyes, the robber fly has three simple eyes in the middle of its head.

The two antennae are short.

Two drumstick shapes called halteres balance the insect during flight.

Scientists think these bristles protect the fly's head when its prey is struggling.

The hairs on its legs help the robber fly to keep hold of its prey in the air.

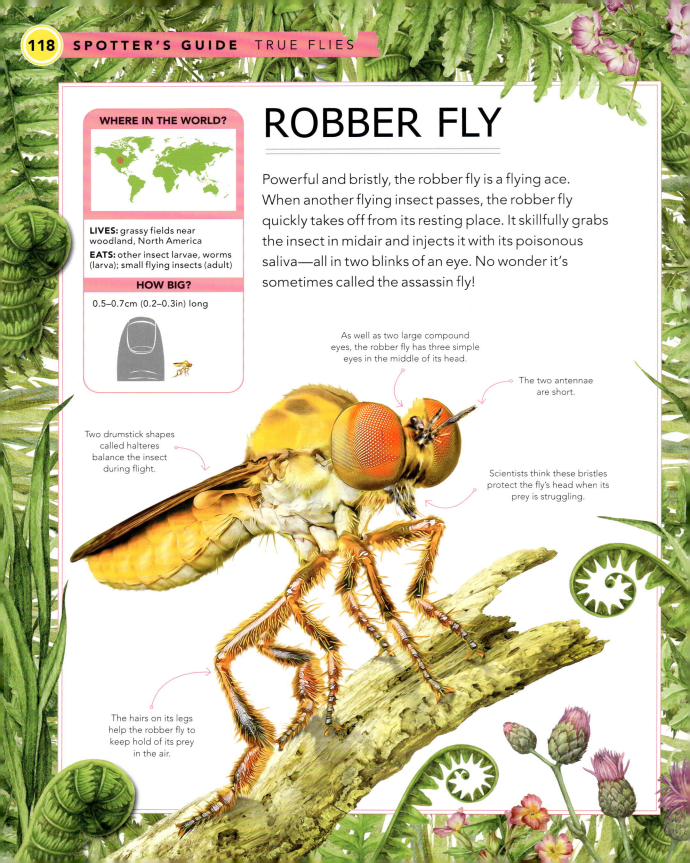

TRUE FLIES **SPOTTER'S GUIDE** 119

HAIRY BEE FLY

WHERE IN THE WORLD?

LIVES: meadows, grassland, heathland, woodland, gardens, worldwide
EATS: flower nectar

HOW BIG?
up to 0.7in (1.8cm) long

This hairy yellowish-brown fly looks like a bumblebee, but it flies in a much more jerky way. You'll spot the fly feeding on the same flowers as the bees.

Bee flies have a very long mouthpart called a proboscis that always sticks out.

Hairy bee fly

TSETSE FLY

WHERE IN THE WORLD?

LIVES: savanna, forests, riverbanks, tropical Africa
EATS: blood

HOW BIG?
0.2–0.6in (0.6–1.6cm) long

This large African fly lives on the blood of both animals and humans. It can cause a serious disease called sleeping sickness.

Tsetse flies fold their wings over their abdomen completely when resting.

The long proboscis points downward as it bites, but it extends directly forward at other times.

Tsetse fly

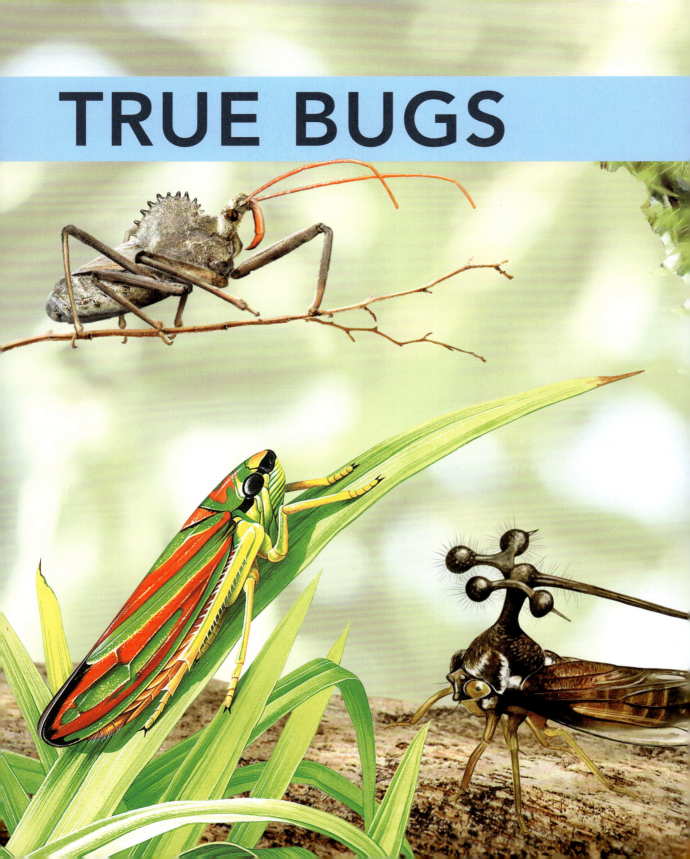
TRUE BUGS

SPOTTER'S GUIDE: TRUE BUGS

HOW TO SPOT TRUE BUGS

We often refer to insects as bugs, but true bugs are a special group that scientists call Hemiptera. True bugs can range in size from the tiny scale insect to the hefty lantern bug. Some jump, some crawl, some hardly move at all, but all share similar features.

LISTEN
If you hear a chirping or whirring sound, you know you are close to a true bug. Look carefully around you to find it.

Study the shape
Look out for unusual shapes such as the oak treehopper's long horn.

TRUE-BUG WATCH

Imagine making a study of just one tree or plant. Which true bugs live here? What do they eat? Are they young nymphs or fully grown adults? Before the trip, research the ones you expect to see.

Learn about eating habits
Most true bugs, such as the oak treehopper, feed on plants. A few are predators that feed on other insects.

Look for movement
True bugs can move around by flying, walking, jumping, or skating over the surface of water. Can you guess how the treehoppper moves?

Watch the behavior
The oak treehopper shakes its body and lets the vibrations travel through the plant—but not all true bugs make noise to communicate.

Oak treehopper

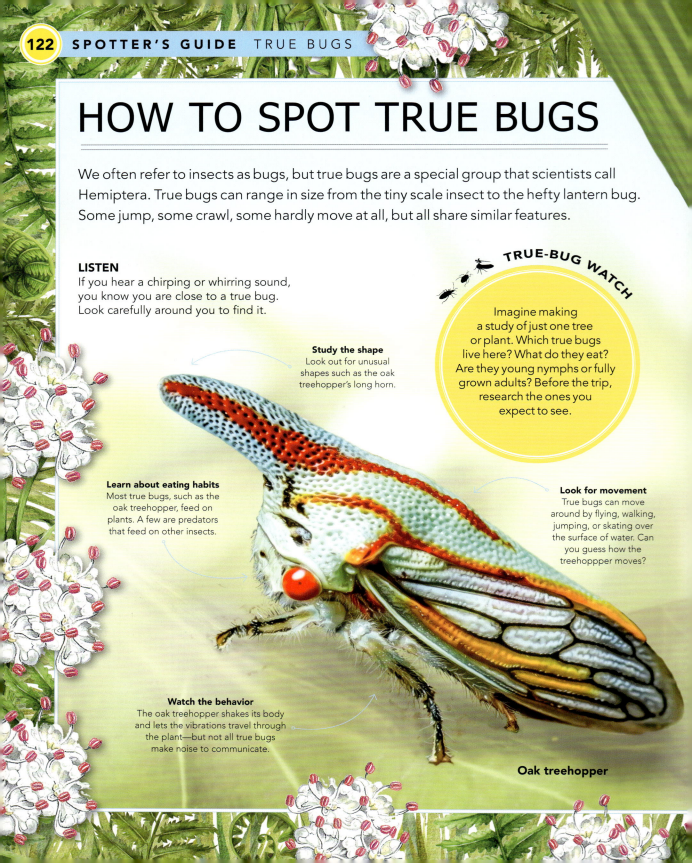

TRUE BUGS **SPOTTER'S GUIDE** 123

WHERE DO TRUE BUGS LIVE?
Most true bugs live on land, but a few live in water. Some, such as the bedbug, can even live in your home!

Minstrel bug

NOISY CHIRPER
Some bugs, like the periodical cicada, make beautiful singing sounds. Listen at night to hear them in action.

Periodical cicada

DON'T EAT ME!
The black-and-red coloring of the minstrel bug is part of its defense. They show predators that it tastes bad.

Black bean aphid

PEST OR NOT?
The black bean aphid can damage plants, so it is seen as a pest. Other insects need it as part of their diet.

WHAT MAKES A TRUE BUG?
Mouthparts: True bugs have piercing, beaklike mouthparts. They use these to suck up liquids such as plant sap or blood.
Wings: True bugs have lacy forewings.
No Metamorphosis: True bugs hatch from the egg as a nymph. The nymphs look similar to the adults but have no wings.
Making sounds: Many true bugs make sounds using their body parts. They do this to "talk" to each other.

SPOTTER'S GUIDE TRUE BUGS

ASSASSIN BUG

If you look on a flower or leaf, you may spot the assassin bug, silent and still. Assassin bugs are ambush predators, which means they wait for another creature to approach them rather than stalking or chasing it. Once it's spied its victim, the assassin bug pounces and injects it with its venom. Game over!

WHERE IN THE WORLD?

LIVES: animal nests, rocks, bark, plants, worldwide
EATS: caterpillars, beetle larvae, other insects

HOW BIG?
0.2–1.6in (0.5–4cm) long

Assassin bugs have a long head and narrow neck.

Assassin bugs have longer legs than other bugs.

Assassin bug

SPOTTER FACT
The assassin bug lives on land. Many other bugs that are predators live in water.

Some assassin bugs will bite humans if they feel threatened. They can pass on a nasty disease.

Assassin bugs are usually black or dark brown. Some also have bright red and orange markings.

TRUE BUGS **SPOTTER'S GUIDE** 125

WHEEL BUG

If you're walking through the countryside and notice a funny smell, you may have disturbed a wheel bug. It uses a stinky whiff to warn off attackers. The wheel bug is a type of assassin bug and is a fierce predator. It gets its name from the wheel shape that sticks up like a cog on its back.

WHERE IN THE WORLD?

LIVES: meadows, woodland, North and Central America
EATS: beetles, moths, grasshoppers

HOW BIG?

1–1.5in (2.5–3.6cm) long

DON'T MISS! Listen for a chirping sound. This is the bug "talking" to others by rubbing its beak against its body.

Beady eyes help the bug spot insects that come its way.

The wheel on its back is the bug's armor, helping to protect it against predators.

Long legs grab the bug's victim and hold it tightly.

The long, pointed beak pierces prey and fills it with venom.

Wheel bug

Insects that are sharp are not easy to eat.

IT'S WILD! Wheel bugs kill their prey very quickly. The insect dies in less than 30 seconds.

SPOTTER'S GUIDE: TRUE BUGS

MILKWEED BUG

WHERE IN THE WORLD?

LIVES: fields, meadows, gardens, parks, North and Central America
EATS: seeds of milkweed plants

HOW BIG?

0.4in (1cm) long

Look closely at a milkweed plant and you'll be sure to spot a group of these pointy-bodied bugs. Their bold red and black colors make them stand out against the green leaves.

Milkweed bug

The bug has a red *X* shape across its back. Sometimes it has white spots at the ends of its wings.

BOX-ELDER BUG

WHERE IN THE WORLD?

LIVES: box elder, maple, and ash trees; North and South America; southern Africa
EATS: leaves and seeds of box elder, maple, and ash trees

HOW BIG?

0.5in (1.3cm) long

Stroll through woodlands to spy the box-elder bug. It likes warmth, so you may see clusters of them sunbathing on a rock.

Box-elder bug

The wings lay flat over the body and slightly overlap.

TRUE BUGS **SPOTTER'S GUIDE** 127

SHIELD BUG

These bugs produce a nasty-smelling liquid that gives them another name—the stink bug! They have lots of different colors and patterns.

WHERE IN THE WORLD?

LIVES: grassland, heathland and moorland, farmland, wetlands, woodland, gardens, worldwide
EATS: sap of plants and trees

HOW BIG?

0.4–0.7in (1–1.7cm) long

These bugs have a hard carapace that is shaped like an old-fashioned shield.

Shield bug

WHERE IN THE WORLD?

LIVES: meadows, roadsides, Europe, North Africa, Middle East
EATS: plants from the carrot family

HOW BIG?

up to 0.5in (1.2cm) long

MINSTREL BUG

Look for plants from the carrot family to spot hordes of these shield bugs. Sometimes there are so many of them that the flowers look red.

The black and red colors are a warning to predators that the bug tastes nasty.

Minstrel bug

SPOTTER'S GUIDE TRUE BUGS

WATER BUGS

Some true bugs have adapted to life in or on the water. Adult aquatic bugs still need to come up for air because they don't have gills like fish. Be careful as you go wading—some of the bugs may mistake your toes for food and give them a little nip!

SPOTTER FACT
The giant water bug hunts small creatures at night. It can sometimes trap bigger things like baby turtles.

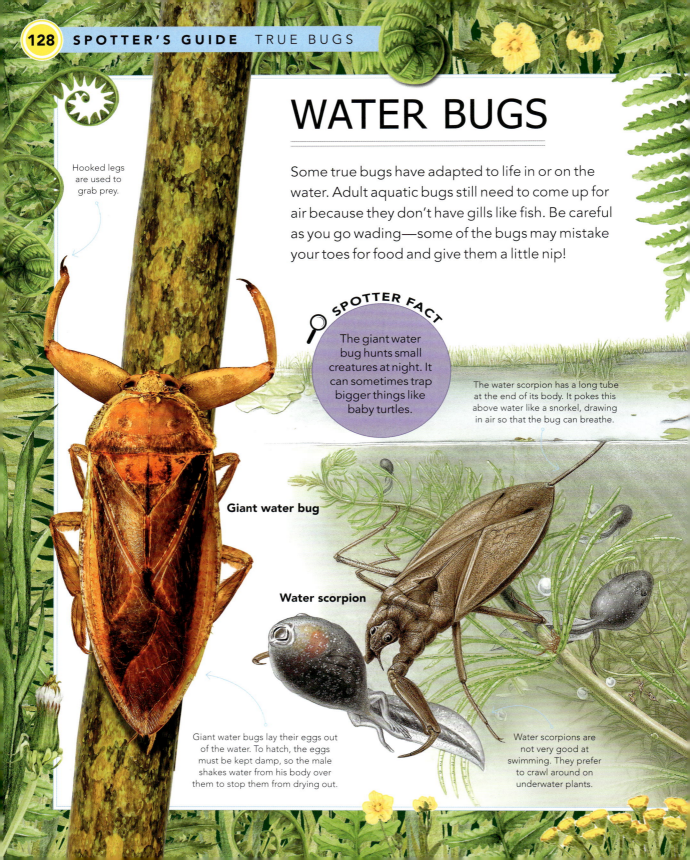

Hooked legs are used to grab prey.

Giant water bug

Water scorpion

The water scorpion has a long tube at the end of its body. It pokes this above water like a snorkel, drawing in air so that the bug can breathe.

Giant water bugs lay their eggs out of the water. To hatch, the eggs must be kept damp, so the male shakes water from his body over them to stop them from drying out.

Water scorpions are not very good at swimming. They prefer to crawl around on underwater plants.

SPOTTER'S GUIDE TRUE BUGS

PERIODICAL CICADA

These bugs get their name because they only emerge in two periods—every thirteen or seventeen years! They spend most of this time as young nymphs underground.

WHERE IN THE WORLD?

LIVES: deciduous woodlands and forests, North America
EATS: tree sap
STATUS: near threatened

HOW BIG?

  1in (2.5cm) long

Males "sing" by vibrating the sides of their bodies. They do this to attract mates.

These cicadas live as adults for four to six weeks.

Periodical cicada

WHERE IN THE WORLD?

LIVES: gardens, parks, farmland, worldwide
EATS: plant sap
STATUS: some species are near threatened to critically endangered

HOW BIG?

 0.1–0.6in (0.3–1.5cm) long

LEAFHOPPER

HOP! Off goes the little leafhopper, using its strong hind legs to escape a predator. If you're quick enough to spot one, you may see it walking sideways, too.

The body is slender and often beautifully colored.

Leafhopper

IT'S WILD! Leafhoppers are often covered with slime. It is water-repellent and protects against predators.

TRUE BUGS **SPOTTER'S GUIDE** 131

MEADOW FROGHOPPER

WHERE IN THE WORLD?

LIVES: gardens, parks, meadows, grassland, open woodland and forests, Europe, Asia, North America, New Zealand
EATS: plant sap

HOW BIG?

nymph 0.2in (0.4–0.6cm); adult 0.2–0.3in (0.5–0.7cm) long

This tiny bug doesn't look much like a frog, but it can certainly hop like one. Froghoppers mostly run and fly to get around, but if they need to, they can jump up to a hundred times longer than their own body length. One big push against the leaf or stem and *boing*! Off they go to find a new place to graze.

Foamy spit hides the pale green nymph from predators and parasites. It also protects it against the heat and cold.

Meadow froghopper nymph

To get their amazing liftoff, froghoppers have tiny spines on their hind legs. These grip the plant they are launching themselves from.

The froghopper holds its wings over its body, giving it the shape of a long oval.

Meadow froghopper

SPOTTER FACT
Females lay their eggs singly or in groups of up to thirty. She produces about four hundred eggs in her lifetime.

COVERED IN SPIT
The froghopper nymph produces a frothy cover made from plant sap. It looks like saliva, or spit, which is why froghoppers are also known as spittlebugs.

SPOTTER'S GUIDE TRUE BUGS

WHERE IN THE WORLD?

LIVES: woodland, forests, parks, US, Brazil, Mexico

EATS: mainly oak tree sap, also birch and chestnut tree sap

HOW BIG?

0.5in (1.3cm) long

OAK TREEHOPPER

These curious-looking bugs live together on oak tree twigs. The males are bright turquoise with red stripes, so they catch the eye as they leap from tree to tree. Watch for the paler gray-and-yellow female, too. Unusually for an insect, she looks after her newborns. If any predators come near the nymphs, she pushes the intruders firmly away.

Oak treehoppers usually have a long frontal "horn." The body is heavy and triangle shaped.

These insects pierce a hole in the tree branches to suck up the sap. They use their saliva to keep the hole moist and stop it from closing up.

SPOTTER FACT

Treehoppers are closely related to leafhoppers. They tend to be larger and have bumps and spines on their bodies.

These treehoppers live together in colonies of fifty to a hundred individuals.

Oak treehoppers have beady red eyes.

Oak treehopper

TRUE BUGS **SPOTTER'S GUIDE** 133

BRAZILIAN TREEHOPPER

This tiny, pea-sized creature might just win the prize for the world's oddest-looking insect! Scientists think the mysterious crown of hairy globes is the treehopper's defense. By making itself look spiky, it puts predators off from eating it. Look out for these minute bugs feeding on the sap of leaves.

WHERE IN THE WORLD?

LIVES: tropical rainforests, Africa, North and South America, Asia, Australia
EATS: plant sap

HOW BIG?

 0.2in (0.6cm) long

The crown is part of the pronotum. This is a body segment just behind an insect's head.

There is a long trailing part behind the crown.

The balls are arranged in a circle above the insect's head.

Treehoppers make vibrations to alert each other to predators, attract a mate, or show a good place to feed.

Brazilian treehopper

SPOTTER FACT

Treehoppers secrete honeydew to feed ants and bees. In return, the ants and bees protect the treehopper from predators.

IT'S WILD! If a predator approaches, the treehopper makes a giant leap to another plant. Otherwise, they don't move around a lot.

134 SPOTTER'S GUIDE TRUE BUGS

LANTERN BUG

Look up to the highest branches in the rainforest to see a lantern bug. This insect is a type of planthopper. It gets its name because people once thought that the long, red "horn" on its head lit up at night. We now know that lantern bugs don't glow in the dark.

The long head part is hollow and curves upward like a rhino's horn. It can be nearly as long as the lantern bug's body.

DON'T MISS! Look on tree trunks and under branches for lines of pale yellow eggs. Females lay a hundred at a time.

WHERE IN THE WORLD?

LIVES: tropical rainforests, Southeast Asia
EATS: green plants, tree sap, fruit

HOW BIG?
1.6–3in (4–8cm) long

The lantern bug often lives on the same tree all its life. Its babies and their babies may stay there, too.

The wings are green with yellow-and-white markings. The lantern bug can fly, but it most often leaps from tree to tree.

Lantern bug

TRUE BUGS **SPOTTER'S GUIDE** 135

SCALE INSECT

WHERE IN THE WORLD?

LIVES: on plant leaves, stems, and roots; tropical and semitropical regions worldwide
EATS: plant sap

HOW BIG?

 0.1–0.2in (0.2–0.4cm) long

If you notice any tiny lumps on plants, chances are they are scale insects. You'll need a magnifying glass to see them properly. They don't really look like animals at all—just little waxy domes on the surface of a stem or leaf.

Scale insects feed by sucking up sap using the mouthparts under their bodies.

Some species of scale insect are both male and female.

SPOTTER FACT
Newly hatched nymphs are called crawlers. They move away from their mother to find their own spot to feed.

The female lays her eggs in a space beneath her body. The nymphs crawl away when they hatch.

The body is covered in a hard, shiny case for protection.

Scale insect

IT'S WILD! Once they have found a place to feed, adult females lose the use of their legs and remain there for the rest of their lives.

136 SPOTTER'S GUIDE TRUE BUGS

BLACK BEAN APHID

This little aphid, also known as a blackfly, is a common sight on plants in the spring and summer. Sometimes, a stem is so completely covered with them that it looks black. These bugs can weaken plants and affect their growth. Some people think aphids are garden pests, but they are a good source of food for many other insects, such as ladybugs and hoverflies.

WHERE IN THE WORLD?

LIVES: soft shoots and leaves, warm areas of Europe, North and South America, Asia, Africa

EATS: plant sap

HOW BIG?

 up to 0.1in (0.1–0.3cm) long

Two tubes at the back produce a waxy liquid. The aphid can spray it over a predator.

Black bean aphid

Aphids don't always have wings. Females can produce winged nymphs, which are able to fly away when the plant becomes overcrowded.

Aphids pierce a plant with their thin mouthparts. They do this so slowly that it can take up to twenty-four hours before they suck up any sap.

IT'S WILD! As well as mating with a male, a female can reproduce alone.

TRUE BUGS **SPOTTER'S GUIDE** 137

WHERE IN THE WORLD?

LIVES: dark, hidden spaces worldwide
EATS: blood

HOW BIG?

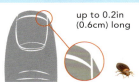

up to 0.2in (0.6cm) long

BEDBUG

Their name tells you that they live in beds, but these little parasites can also hide in other dark spaces—even under wallpaper. Bedbugs survive on blood, piercing the skin with their mouthparts and injecting a mixture of chemicals that keeps the blood flowing. Ten minutes later, the bedbug has finished its tasty meal.

Before a meal, the bedbug's body is flat and oval.

Colors range from light brown to a deeper reddish-brown after feeding.

Females can lay up to five hundred eggs in their lifetime.

Bedbug

Bedbugs only need to feed every five to seven days.

IT'S WILD! Bedbugs hatch as nymphs. They molt, or shed their skin, five times before becoming adults.

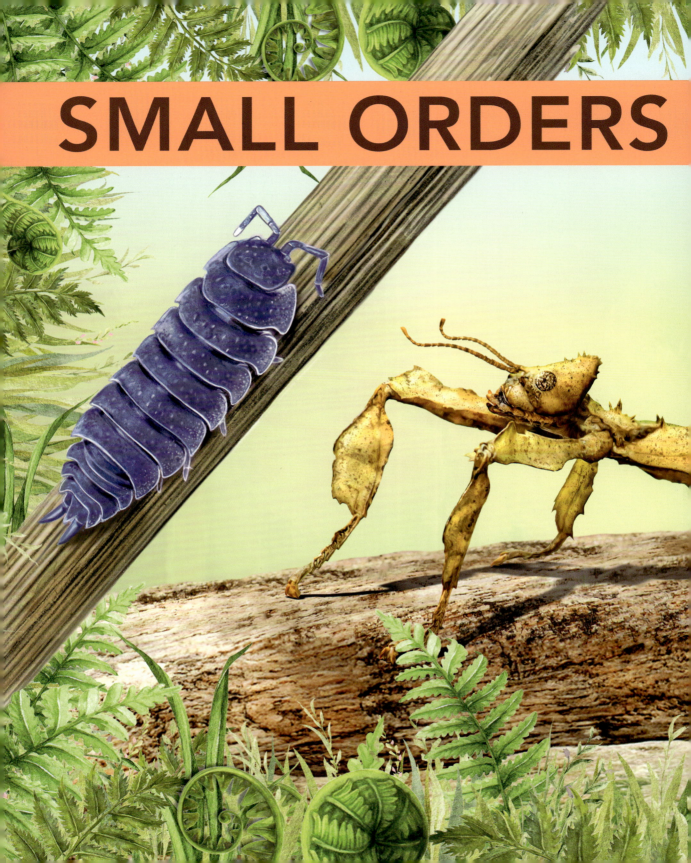

SMALL ORDERS

SPOTTER'S GUIDE: SMALL ORDERS

HOW TO SPOT SMALL ORDERS

Scientists organize bugs into about thirty major groups called orders, according to things the insects have in common. Some of these orders have only a small number of bug types in them. These groups are known as small orders. We have put some of them together in this chapter, alongside some common bugs you may come across in freshwater pools. You'll find all sorts of very different creatures.

LOOK CLOSELY
Study a bug carefully. Remember that some mimic creatures that are more dangerous than they are.

SMALL ORDERS WATCH
Imagine you're out and about, studying lots of different types of bugs. Make a list of all those you find. How are they different? Do they have things in common? Look up the groups they belong to.

Look at the body
The scorpionfly looks a bit like a real scorpion. It is harmless—but other predators stay away, just in case.

Scorpionfly

Notice the wings
How they hold their wings is a good way to tell one species apart from another. The scorpionfly's wings are held across its body.

Count the legs
Some bugs in the small orders have six legs, but others have many more.

142 SPOTTER'S GUIDE SMALL ORDERS

DRAGONFLY

Zip! A dragonfly zooms past your head, snatching little bugs out of the air with its legs. You've just had a close encounter with one of the largest and fastest flying insects in the world. Dragonflies need warmth to fly. Look out for them basking in the sunshine and whirring their wings to make more heat.

Dragonflies catch insects in midair by scooping them up in a basket shape they make with their legs.

Large eyes wrap around the dragonfly's head and usually touch at the top. Each eye has about 24,000 tiny lenses.

There is often a narrow "waist" at the top of the abdomen.

Dragonfly

A dragonfly rests with its lacy wings spread out. This is one way to tell it apart from its close relative, the damselfly.

Many species have bright, metallic colors.

The hindwings are usually shorter and broader than the forewings.

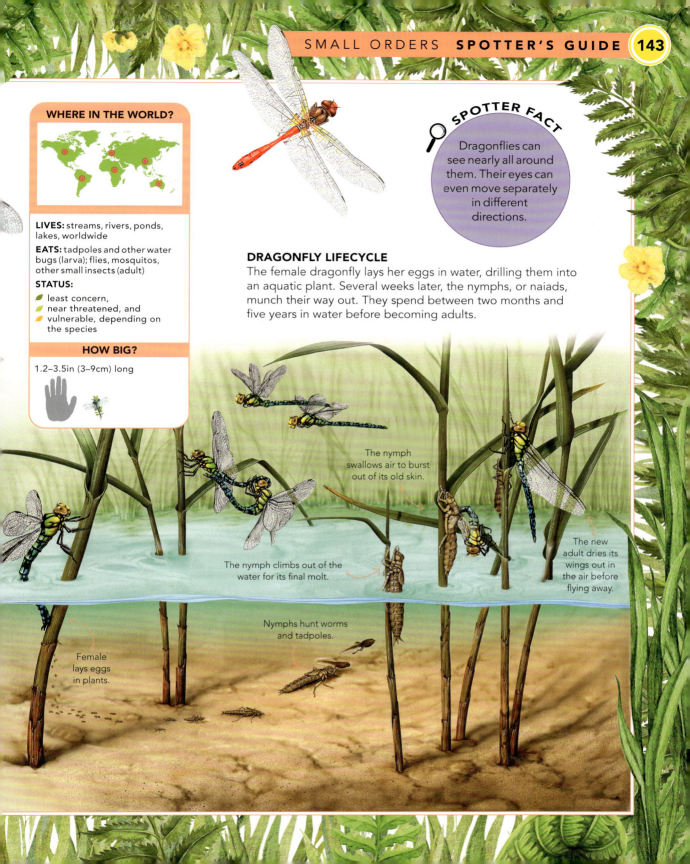

144 SPOTTER'S GUIDE SMALL ORDERS

BANDED DEMOISELLE

The banded demoiselle is named after the dark band on the males' wings. It is a type of damselfly. These insects are related to dragonflies, but they are smaller and more delicate and fold their wings over their back when resting. If you search near slow-flowing streams and rivers, you'll see the males fluttering around, showing themselves off to females.

WHERE IN THE WORLD?

LIVES: streams, rivers, Europe, Asia
EATS: insects
STATUS: least concern

HOW BIG?
1.9in (4.8cm) long

Males are territorial. This means they chase off other insects from their chosen area.

The male demoiselle is bluish-green. The female is pale metallic green with see-through wings.

A damselfly's forewings and hindwings are the same shape.

The dark spot or band covers the outer part of the male demoiselle's wings.

Banded demoiselle

SPOTTER FACT
The banded demoiselle needs clean water to thrive. It is not threatened yet, but it is very sensitive to pollution.

SMALL ORDERS **SPOTTER'S GUIDE** 145

EASTERN DOBSONFLY

WHERE IN THE WORLD?

LIVES: rocky streams and rivers, North America
EATS: insects, small fish (larva); no food (adult)

HOW BIG?
3–5.5in (7.5–14cm) long

You'll have to be out and about on a summer night to spot dobsonflies. This is when these large insects mate and lay eggs. Males fight each other using their long, hornlike mouthparts for the right to mate with a female. A good place to see these jousting tournaments is by fast-flowing rivers and streams.

Male dobsonflies live for about three days, the females for ten. They must quickly find a mate during this time.

The wings overlap slightly when at rest.

The males' long mouthparts can give a painful but harmless bite.

The scientific name for this order, or group, of insects means "large wing."

Eastern dobsonfly

During the day, dobsonflies hide in dense plants and bushes near streams.

SPOTTER FACT
Dobsonflies don't need to eat. They survive on what they have eaten during the larval stage.

SPOTTER'S GUIDE SMALL ORDERS

LACEWING

It's easy to see how the lacewing got its name. Just look at those delicate, see-through wings! The veins running through the wings make them look like the most intricate piece of lace. Watch as they catch the light in the sunshine.

Lacewing

The eyes are shiny and brass-colored. This gives the insect its nickname of goldeneye.

A gland gives off a nasty smell when the lacewing is threatened.

The four wings are roughly the same size.

DON'T MISS!
The common lacewing hibernates in buildings for the winter. See if you can spot one in your home.

CLEVER CAMOUFLAGE
Some lacewing larvae cover themselves with little bits of sand, leaf, and even other insects—dead or alive. This disguise means they are protected from predators and can hunt their prey without being noticed.

Lacewing larva

WHERE IN THE WORLD?

LIVES: grassland, wetland, farmland, urban, worldwide
EATS: aphids and other small insects

HOW BIG?
0.6in (1.5cm) long

SMALL ORDERS **SPOTTER'S GUIDE** 147

ANTLION

Antlions look like a cross between a lacewing and a dragonfly. You can tell them apart from those insects by looking for clubbed antennae. Antlions get their name because of their larvae, which have enormous jaws like a lion and love to eat ants.

WHERE IN THE WORLD?

LIVES: sand dunes, heathland, grassland, scrubland, rocky slopes, worldwide

EATS: ants (larva); insects, pollen, nectar (adult)

HOW BIG?

2.3–4in (6–10cm) long

The long antennae end in clubs.

SPOTTER FACT

The larva digs a pit and hides under loose soil. It darts out to grab ants when they fall in.

Adult antlions are nocturnal. They fly around slowly at night.

The wingspan can be more than 4in (10cm) from tip to tip.

Antlions fold their wings along their bodies when they rest.

Antlion

148 SPOTTER'S GUIDE SMALL ORDERS

CADDISFLY

It's easy to mistake the hairy-winged caddisfly for a moth—they are closely related. Unlike moths, these insects gather by water and fly in swarms above the surface. They have flimsy wings, which means their flight isn't very strong. When caddisflies rest, their wings form a roof over their bodies.

WHERE IN THE WORLD?

LIVES: ponds, lakes, rivers, worldwide
EATS: flower nectar or no food

HOW BIG?
0.1–1.2in (0.3–3cm) long

DON'T MISS!
Look underwater for a moving shelter. The larva carries this protection around with it while it hunts for food.

Most adults only live for a short time and so don't need to eat.

Caddisflies are weak fliers, but they have been known to fly 3 miles (5km) or more.

Caddisfly wings are covered in little hairs. A moth's wings have scales.

Caddisfly

BUILDING A SHELTER
Caddisfly larvae grow up in water. Most build shelters to protect themselves by spinning together sand, leaves, twigs, and stones with silk they make in their mouth. Some species build these shelters only when they are ready to become a pupa.

Larva with shelter

Pupa

SMALL ORDERS **SPOTTER'S GUIDE** 149

THRIP

The tiny, slender thrip is sometimes called a thunderfly because it is often seen before a thunderstorm. It loves warm, damp weather.

SPOTTER FACT

Some species of thrip carry diseases that damage plants. Others are helpful pollinators.

The wings are fringed and feathery.

Thrip

WHERE IN THE WORLD?

LIVES: farmland, gardens, buildings, worldwide
EATS: plant sap, fungi

HOW BIG?

0.1in (0.2cm) long

MAYFLY

This delicate-looking insect flies around at night in great swarms. Mayflies often hatch together on a single day in summer—not just in May.

WHERE IN THE WORLD?

LIVES: lakes, rivers, worldwide
EATS: no food

HOW BIG?

0.6–1.2in (1.5–3cm) long

Mayfly

Lacy wings are triangle shaped and transparent.

The long tails are called filaments.

150 **SPOTTER'S GUIDE** SMALL ORDERS

STONEFLY

If you see a stonefly while walking along a fast-flowing stream or river, it's a sign that the water is clean. Stoneflies are very sensitive to pollution. These short-lived insects look a bit like lacewings, but their closest relative is the mayfly.

WHERE IN THE WORLD?

LIVES: streams, ponds, worldwide
EATS: plants, small insects

HOW BIG?

0.2–2.3in (0.6–6cm) long

Stoneflies are often found on rocks and stones, which is how they get their name.

The sturdy legs end in claws.

When the stonefly is resting, its transparent wings fold flat like a fan.

Stoneflies have two long tail bristles.

SPOTTER FACT
Stoneflies find each other by "drumming." They tap the end of their abdomens against the ground using different rhythms.

SMALL ORDERS **SPOTTER'S GUIDE** 151

SCORPIONFLY

WHERE IN THE WORLD?

LIVES: hedgerows, thick vegetation, North America, Europe, Asia
EATS: dead insects, nectar, rotting fruit

HOW BIG?

0.6–0.8in (1.5–2cm) long

Don't be afraid! The male scorpionfly has a tail that looks like a scorpion's stinger, but unlike its namesake, this insect is completely harmless to humans. The scorpionfly is closely related to the flea, even though it looks more like a true fly. Peek into hedgerows and bushes to find it.

SPOTTER FACT
The abdomen of the female scorpionfly is different from the male's. It is straight and narrows toward the tip.

Only the males have the upturned tail that gives the insect its name.

The antennae are long and threadlike.

The scorpionfly has a long rostrum, or beak.

Scorpionfly

The abdomen has eleven segments.

IT'S WILD! Scorpionflies are scavengers. This means they feed on things that are already dead.

152 SPOTTER'S GUIDE SMALL ORDERS

STICK INSECT

WHERE IN THE WORLD?

LIVES: hedgerows, gardens, thick vegetation, worldwide
EATS: plants

HOW BIG?

0.8–25in (2–64cm) long

Wait a minute—did that twig just move? No—you're looking at a stick insect, a creature with the most remarkable camouflage! Colored brown or green, stick insects have long, narrow bodies that look just like the twigs and stems of plants. They are usually out at night, feeding on bushes.

Stick insects prefer warm, damp climates.

Stick insects have compound eyes that can see well in the dark.

Stick insect

SPOTTER FACT

Stick insects don't undergo metamorphosis. The offspring look like a smaller version of the adult.

The other name for this bug is ghost insect. This is because it is so well camouflaged, it is hard to see.

IT'S WILD! One stick insect, of a Chinese species, measured 25in (64cm) long. It is the world's longest insect.

SMALL ORDERS **SPOTTER'S GUIDE** 153

SPINY LEAF STICK INSECT

Many species of stick insect look almost exactly like twigs, but this one resembles a scrunched-up old leaf. The clever spiny leaf stick insect disguises itself even further by swaying back and forth in the breeze, just like real leaves do. If a predator approaches, it curls its tail over its back to look like a deadly scorpion.

WHERE IN THE WORLD?

LIVES: forests, grassland, northeastern Australia
EATS: eucalyptus and other leaves
STATUS: least concern

HOW BIG?

 female 8in (20cm); male 4in (10cm) long

SPOTTER FACT

Scientists are discovering new types of stick insect all the time. At present, there are three thousand species worldwide.

The female has very small wings but is too heavy to fly. The males have longer wings and can fly away to escape danger.

Thorny spines on the female's body help defend her from predators.

These stick insects can give off a nasty smell to make predators leave them alone.

Spiny leaf stick insect

IT'S WILD! Female stick insects can reproduce without a male. All the offspring will be female.

SPOTTER'S GUIDE SMALL ORDERS

EARWIG

This nocturnal creature gets its name because its hindwings look like human ears when they are unfolded—not because it lives in your ears. Look for it in small crevices.

Earwig

The pincers can trap or kill prey, but they are mainly used in defense.

WHERE IN THE WORLD?

LIVES: gardens, farmland, buildings, worldwide
EATS: plants, ripe fruit, aphids, spiders, insect eggs

HOW BIG?

0.4–0.6in (1–1.5cm) long

FIELD GRASSHOPPER

Listen out for little chirps on your daytime walk. If you look closely, you'll see a solitary male grasshopper rubbing his legs against his wings to create this beautiful song for his mate.

Grasshoppers are related to crickets, but grasshoppers have shorter antennae.

Field grasshopper

WHERE IN THE WORLD?

LIVES: dry grassland, shrubland, mountain slopes, gardens, Europe
EATS: plants
STATUS:
🌿 least concern

HOW BIG?

0.6–1in (1.5–2.5cm) long

SMALL ORDERS **SPOTTER'S GUIDE** 155

LOCUST

The sky suddenly darkens. If you look up, you can see an enormous swarm of locusts! Locusts and grasshoppers look the same, but unlike grasshoppers, locusts live in large groups. When the weather is very warm and dry, they can breed very quickly and fly in a great cloud together. Locusts eat any plants they settle on and can strip a field of crops in no time at all.

WHERE IN THE WORLD?

LIVES: farmland, sand dunes, Central and South America, Africa, Asia, Australia, Europe
EATS: plants
STATUS:
 least concern

HOW BIG?
female 2–2.7in (5–7cm); male 1.2–1.7in (3–4.5cm) long

There are no physical differences between a grasshopper and a locust. The name changes when they gather together in groups.

SPOTTER FACT
Locusts cause famines. Scientists are finding environmentally friendly ways to stop locusts from destroying crops.

Locusts are strong fliers and can travel huge distances.

Locust

SWIRLING SWARM
A swarm containing billions of locusts can spread out over thousands of square miles. This is known as a plague of locusts because of the harm they cause to important food crops.

IT'S WILD! Locusts are eaten as food in many cultures. They are very nutritious.

SPOTTER'S GUIDE SMALL ORDERS

JERUSALEM CRICKET

The Jerusalem cricket has a curious name. It isn't really a cricket, and it doesn't come from Jerusalem! It does have a song like crickets do, which it makes by drumming its abdomen on the ground. You'll find it at night burrowing into the earth to eat plant roots.

WHERE IN THE WORLD?

LIVES: sandy soil, US, Mexico, Central America
EATS: plant roots and tubers, other insects
STATUS: vulnerable

HOW BIG?

1.2–3in (3–7.5cm) long

IN DANGER

This species often lives on sandy shores. They are threatened when the coastline erodes in bad weather.

SPOTTER FACT

The mandibles, or mouthparts, are strong. They can cut through plastic and material and give a painful bite.

The striped body is humpbacked.

The cricket gives off a nasty smell when threatened.

The feet help the cricket to dig in the ground.

Jerusalem cricket

The Jerusalem cricket is also known as the potato bug because it likes to eat plant tubers such as potatoes.

SMALL ORDERS **SPOTTER'S GUIDE** 157

FIELD CRICKET

Crouch down to spot the field cricket in its burrow in the ground. Its shiny black body stands out against the brown earth.

WHERE IN THE WORLD?

LIVES: grassland, worldwide
EATS: plants, other insects
STATUS:
 endangered in some countries

HOW BIG?

0.7–1in (1.7–2.5cm) long

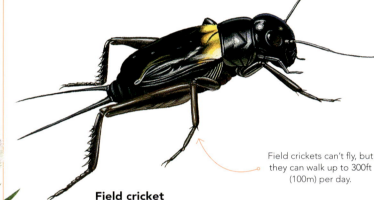

Field crickets can't fly, but they can walk up to 300ft (100m) per day.

Field cricket

GREAT GREEN BUSH CRICKET

WHERE IN THE WORLD?

LIVES: shrubland, grassland, meadows, parks, gardens, Europe, West Asia
EATS: other insects
STATUS:
 least concern

HOW BIG?

1.6–2.2in (4–5.5cm) long

On a late afternoon stroll, listen for the male bush cricket's loud song. It sounds a bit like a sewing machine and carries on well into the night.

Great green bush cricket

The female lays eggs using a long body part called an ovipositor.

SPOTTER'S GUIDE SMALL ORDERS

BROAD-WINGED KATYDID

You'll need keen eyesight to spot a katydid, or bush cricket. This grasshopper-like insect has such good camouflage that it merges with the leaves it eats. You'll easily hear the clicking sounds the male makes to win a mate. He rubs one wing against the other, repeating the clicks every few minutes.

WHERE IN THE WORLD?

LIVES: woodland, North America
EATS: leaves, flowers, fruit

HOW BIG?

2–2.5in (5–6.5cm) long

DON'T MISS!

The male katydid has three different "songs." Listen in the day, at dusk, and during the night to hear them.

- The long hind legs have thick upper parts to help the katydid to jump.
- The wings have veins running through them, just like leaves do.
- By leaving gaps in his "song," the male disguises exactly where he is. This protects him from any nearby predators.
- Long antennae help the insect feel and smell what's around it.
- Katydids have a kind of ear on their front knees so that they can hear the sounds they make.

Broad-winged katydid

SMALL ORDERS **SPOTTER'S GUIDE** 159

HEAD LOUSE

WHERE IN THE WORLD?

LIVES: human head, worldwide
EATS: blood

HOW BIG?

approx. 0.1in (0.2–0.3cm) long

The head louse is a parasite—it lives on a host, or another animal. This tiny creature lives on human heads, feeding on blood from the scalp. Not everyone has them, but look among the hairs to see. You might also spot lots of sticky white balls. These are empty egg cases that nymphs, or young lice, have hatched from.

Female head lice lay six to ten eggs per day. They glue them to the hair shaft close to the scalp.

Lice live for about thirty days.

SPOTTER FACT
Head lice can't jump or fly. They can quickly move to another person when heads touch.

Lice make the head feel itchy. This is a reaction to their bites.

Lice feed several times per day by sucking blood. They inject a chemical into the skin to keep the blood flowing while they drink.

Hooks at the end of the legs grip the hairs. This makes the louse hard to remove.

Head louse

IT'S WILD! Head lice die after one or two days if they are not living on a human head.

SPOTTER'S GUIDE SMALL ORDERS

HUMAN FLEA

This little parasite can be found on people, but it also lives on other large mammals. Its bites cause the skin to swell up into little itchy bumps. If you look carefully, you may witness its most amazing ability—this flea can jump up to 150 times its height. That's like you jumping over a very tall skyscraper!

WHERE IN THE WORLD?

LIVES: large mammals, homes, farms, animals' nests, worldwide (except Arctic)
EATS: flea droppings (larva); blood (adult)

HOW BIG?
approx. 0.1in (0.2–0.3cm) long

SPOTTER FACT
Females lay twenty to fifty eggs per day. They can lay up to two thousand eggs in their lifetime.

Without a magnifying glass, fleas look like little black specks.

Adults suck blood ten to fifteen times per day. They can also go for one to two weeks without eating.

Elastic pads on their back legs act like a springboard for the flea. It can jump several times in a row.

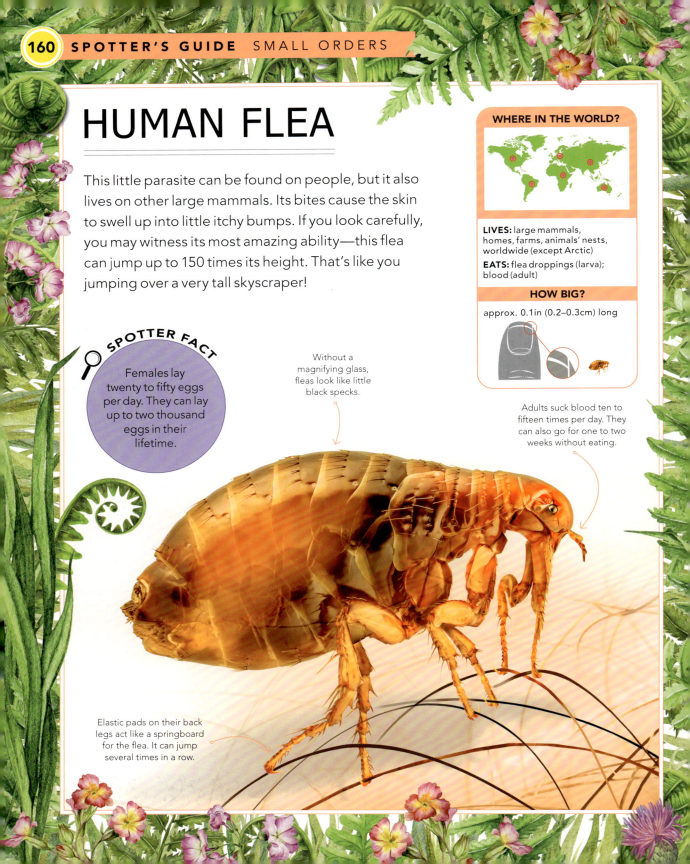

SMALL ORDERS **SPOTTER'S GUIDE** 161

CAT FLEA

This parasite begins its life as a larva, living in dark places. When it hatches as an adult, it finds its host—a cat or dog—by sensing the animal's body heat and the air it breathes out. It jumps on to the animal and hides in its thick fur, ready to start feeding on its blood.

WHERE IN THE WORLD?

LIVES: cat and dog fur, worldwide
EATS: blood

HOW BIG?

approx. 0.1in (0.1–0.2cm) long

Cat fleas can jump about 8in (20cm).

A sharp mouthpart called a proboscis pierces the animal's skin so that it can suck up blood.

The flea's body is very flat. This helps it slide through the animal's thick coat.

Cat flea

Backward-facing bristles get caught on the animal's hair. This stops the flea from being brushed away when the animal is grooming itself.

SPOTTER FACT
Larvae eat the droppings of adult fleas and any eggs that have fallen off the cat or dog.

IT'S WILD! Fleas have existed for millions of years. Fossils found in China show that even the dinosaurs had them!

SPOTTER'S GUIDE: SMALL ORDERS

MANTISES

Mantises are some of nature's most unusual-looking insects. Their long front legs and upright posture makes them seem strangely human. The ancient Egyptians and ancient Greeks even thought they had magical powers. We know differently today, but that doesn't make mantises any less fascinating.

WHERE IN THE WORLD?

LIVES: shrubland, grassland, tropical grassland and forests, savanna, deserts, urban
- European mantis: Europe, Asia, Africa, North America
- Devil's flower mantis: East Africa
- Orchid mantis: Southeast Asia
- Texas unicorn mantis: southern US, Mexico, northern South America

EATS: crickets, flies, moths, butterflies, beetles, bees
STATUS:
- least concern

HOW BIG?

 European mantis 2.3–3.5in (6–9cm) long

 Devil's flower mantis 4–5in (10–13cm) long

 Orchid mantis female 3in (7cm) long; male 1in (2.5cm) long

 Texas unicorn mantis up to 3in (7cm) long

The long front legs are held as if the insect is praying. This gives the insect its common name—praying mantis.

SPOTTER FACT
Many animals have colors and markings that match their surroundings. This is called mimicry.

Mantises are ferocious predators. They catch prey with their spiked front legs.

SPOTTER FACT
The female sometimes bites the head off the male while mating. She may eat the rest of him afterward.

European mantis

SMALL ORDERS **SPOTTER'S GUIDE** 163

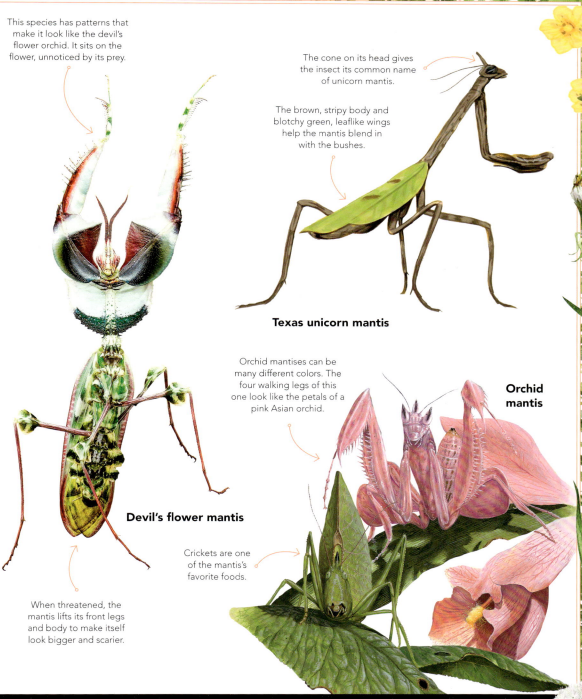

This species has patterns that make it look like the devil's flower orchid. It sits on the flower, unnoticed by its prey.

The cone on its head gives the insect its common name of unicorn mantis.

The brown, stripy body and blotchy green, leaflike wings help the mantis blend in with the bushes.

Texas unicorn mantis

Orchid mantises can be many different colors. The four walking legs of this one look like the petals of a pink Asian orchid.

Orchid mantis

Devil's flower mantis

Crickets are one of the mantis's favorite foods.

When threatened, the mantis lifts its front legs and body to make itself look bigger and scarier.

IT'S WILD! A newborn flower mantis looks like a stinging ant. As it grows, the nymph starts to resemble a dead leaf.

SPOTTER'S GUIDE SMALL ORDERS

AMERICAN COCKROACH

If you see or hear something scuttle across the floor, it might be a cockroach. These creatures can move very quickly, using their fast legs rather than their wings to escape danger. Cockroaches have been around for 300 million years, making them one of nature's most amazing survivors.

WHERE IN THE WORLD?

LIVES: buildings, sewers, drains, wood piles, gardens, worldwide

EATS: food scraps, insects, decaying leaves, fungi

HOW BIG?

1.3–2.1in (3.2–5.3cm) long

DON'T MISS! Watch as the cockroach grooms its antennae. Despite living in dirty places, cockroaches keep themselves very clean.

The long antennae can "smell" what's around, including other cockroaches.

The carapace, or outer body, is hard and shiny.

American cockroach

Cockroaches can squeeze themselves through gaps by flattening their bodies and spreading their legs out.

IT'S WILD! Cockroaches have many predators. They are an important food for other animals.

SMALL ORDERS **SPOTTER'S GUIDE** 165

TERMITES

If you come across an enormous mound of earth, you know termites have been at work. The towers are so big that some people call them cathedrals. Termites live in large colonies, or groups, inside the mounds. Each has a job to do, so the different types are called workers and soldiers. They are ruled by a king and queen.

WHERE IN THE WORLD?

LIVES: forests: grassland
- Soil termite: Southeast Asia
- Damp-wood termite: Pacific Northwest of North America
- Spinifex termite: Australia

EATS: wood, leaves, mushrooms, grass

HOW BIG?

 Soil termite 0.2–2.5in (0.5–6cm) long

 Damp-wood termite 0.7in (1.8cm) long

 Spinifex termite 0.1–0.2 in (0.3–0.5cm) long

The worker termites are pale. They are sometimes called white ants.

Soldiers have a dark-brown head and long snout.

Soil termite

Spinifex termite

TERMITE MOUNDS
Mounds are made from soil and chewed wood, glued together with saliva, or spit. They can be well over 20ft (7m) tall.

Inside the mound is a hollow chamber where the workers grow mushrooms to eat.

This type of termite is found inside damp or rotting wood.

Damp-wood termite

166 SPOTTER'S GUIDE SMALL ORDERS

WOODLOUSE

WHERE IN THE WORLD?

LIVES: grassland, heathland, woodland, parks, gardens, Europe
EATS: dead plants and small creatures, fungi

HOW BIG? 0.5in (1.4cm) long

Pick up a stone or piece of wood in your garden or local park and you'll probably find a woodlouse. This little creature likes to hide in warm, damp places to stop itself from drying out. The woodlouse looks like it's dressed in shiny gray armor. When threatened, some species curl up into a ball using this exoskeleton, or hard outer body, to protect themselves.

Even though they are called woodlice, they are not parasites like real lice are.

The thorax is made up of seven segments. This makes it easier for the woodlouse to move around.

Woodlouse

There are seven pairs of jointed legs.

SPOTTER FACT
Woodlice eat pretty much anything they find. When they poop, important nutrients are returned to the soil.

IT'S WILD! Woodlice are crustaceans. They are more closely related to shrimps and lobsters than to land-dwelling bugs.

SMALL ORDERS **SPOTTER'S GUIDE** 167

SILVERFISH

This wingless insect gets its name from its light-gray color. It lives on land rather than water, so it isn't a fish at all—but it does have silvery scales and move a little bit like one. Silverfish like damp places, so look for them under your sink or bathtub.

SPOTTER FACT
Silverfish are one of the oldest insects. They existed at the time of the very first land plants, long before the dinosaurs.

Silverfish are nocturnal. They hide in dark places during the day.

Like most animals, silverfish need carbohydrates in their diet. Unlike others, they are able to digest the starchy cellulose in paper and glue.

As they move about, silverfish waggle from side to side like a fish.

Tiny scales come off if you touch them.

There are three tail bristles.

WHERE IN THE WORLD?

LIVES: damp areas in buildings, worldwide
EATS: paper, carpets, clothing, glue, hair, cereals

HOW BIG?
0.5–1in (1.3–2.5cm) long

SPOTTER'S GUIDE SMALL ORDERS

168

SPRINGTAIL

Get a magnifying glass and have a gentle dig in damp soil. If you're lucky, you'll spot a springtail. It may catch your eye because of its giant leaps. These tiny creatures get their name because of a tail-like part that is folded under their bodies. When it's released, it whacks the ground and makes the creature spring into the air.

WHERE IN THE WORLD?

LIVES: soil, worldwide, including Antarctica and Greenland

EATS: decaying plants, fungi, algae

HOW BIG?

up to 0.1in (0.3cm) long

SPOTTER FACT

The body contains chemicals that stop the springtail from freezing. This means it can survive in very cold climates.

Springtails can jump about a hundred times their body length to escape predators.

This type of springtail has a very round body and two long antennae.

Even though it has six legs, a springtail isn't an insect. It's part of a bigger group of animals called hexapods.

Springtail

IT'S WILD!
At the end of its jump, the springtail curves into a *U* shape to stop itself from flipping over.

SMALL ORDERS **SPOTTER'S GUIDE** 169

CENTIPEDE

This creature's name means "100 feet." It never has this number, though, so there's no point in counting to check. It will quickly run away before you could even try.

WHERE IN THE WORLD?

LIVES: grassland, heathland, woodland, parks, gardens, worldwide

EATS: insects, spiders, slugs, worms, flies

HOW BIG?

0.7–1.2in (1.8–3cm) long

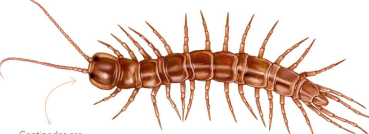

Centipedes are predators. They have a venomous bite.

Centipede

MILLIPEDE

WHERE IN THE WORLD?

LIVES: shrubland, grassland, woodland, worldwide

EATS: dead plants, fungus, animal droppings

HOW BIG?

0.8–1.7in (2–4.5cm) long

Take care not to disturb this slow-moving creature. Millipedes curl up into a ball if they feel threatened.

Millipedes have two pairs of legs on the underside of each body segment.

Millipede

SPOTTER'S GUIDE: SMALL ORDERS

CARIDEAN SHRIMP

Many aquatic creatures release their eggs into water, but this crustacean broods them in sacs under her body. Look for her in fresh water.

WHERE IN THE WORLD?

LIVES: fresh water, worldwide
EATS: plankton, algae

HOW BIG?

0.5–12in (1.2–30cm) long

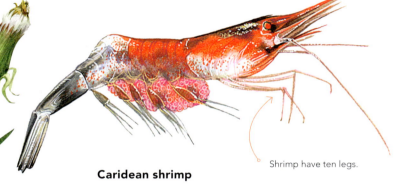

Caridean shrimp

Shrimp have ten legs.

TANAID

WHERE IN THE WORLD?

LIVES: muddy seashores, Singapore
EATS: unknown (this species); tiny bits of dead plants and animals (other species)

HOW BIG?

approx. 0.1in (0.2–0.3cm) long

This tiny crustacean looks like a long shrimp with very short legs. Spot this species on muddy shores around the island of Singapore.

Tanaid

Tanaids usually have very large front claws for burrowing in mud.

SMALL ORDERS **SPOTTER'S GUIDE** 171

WATER FLEA

If you look closely in a freshwater pool, you may just be able to see a water flea. If you use a magnifying glass, you'll notice that it's completely see-through. This means you can see inside its body. Look again and you'll see it has just one eye.

WHERE IN THE WORLD?

LIVES: still fresh water, northern hemisphere

EATS: algae, bacteria, dead plant matter

HOW BIG?

up to 0.2in (0.5cm) long

Eggs are stored in an area called a brood chamber.

The flea feeds on algae and tiny bits of plants floating in the water.

Water fleas are not strong enough to swim against the current in flowing water.

The flea has a carapace.

SPOTTER FACT

This water flea is a crustacean. It is related to shrimp, crabs, lobsters, and crayfish.

172 SPOTTER'S GUIDE SMALL ORDERS

OSTRACOD

Take a small sample of fresh water from a pond and look at it through a magnifying glass. Can you see little seed-shaped creatures swimming about? They are ostracods, or seed shrimp. These miniature crustaceans have a carapace that is split into two halves like a clam shell. The hinge is along the center of the ostracod's back.

WHERE IN THE WORLD?

LIVES: fresh water, Asia
EATS: tiny pieces of dead animals and plants, algae

HOW BIG?

less than 0.1in (0.1cm) long

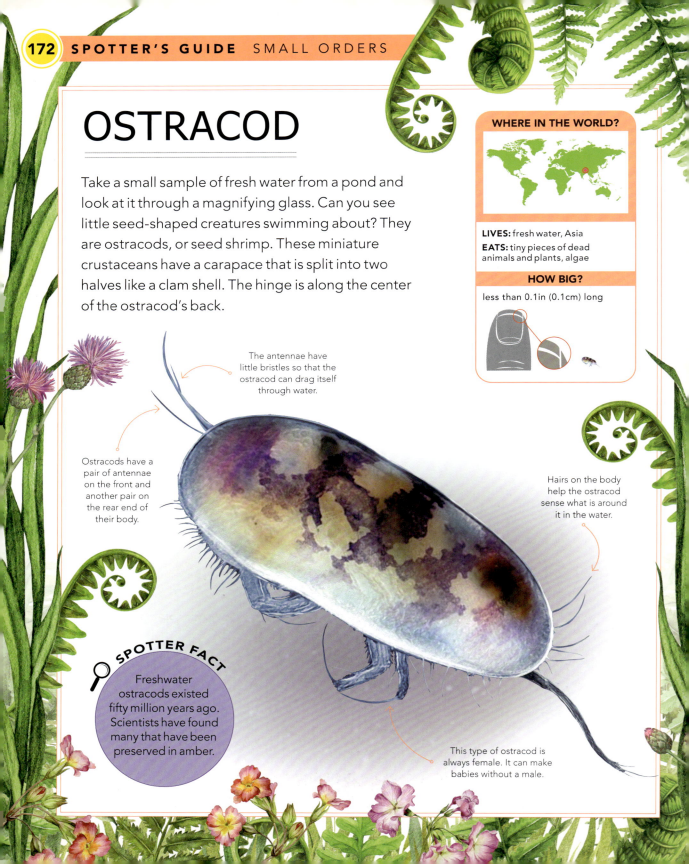

The antennae have little bristles so that the ostracod can drag itself through water.

Ostracods have a pair of antennae on the front and another pair on the rear end of their body.

Hairs on the body help the ostracod sense what is around it in the water.

SPOTTER FACT
Freshwater ostracods existed fifty million years ago. Scientists have found many that have been preserved in amber.

This type of ostracod is always female. It can make babies without a male.

SMALL ORDERS   **SPOTTER'S GUIDE**   173

CYCLOPS COPEPOD

It's hard to believe this little creature is related to crabs and lobsters. Like them, it is a crustacean. Tiny aquatic animals like copepods are known as zooplankton. They are an important food for many bigger creatures. This copepod species is called cyclops. It has just one eye and is named after the one-eyed giant in Greek mythology.

WHERE IN THE WORLD?

LIVES: slow-moving or still fresh water, worldwide, including polar regions
EATS: algae, other plankton

HOW BIG?

 up to 0.2in (0.5cm) long

The eye is usually red, but it can also be black.

Like all crustaceans, the copepod has a carapace.

This creature is so small that its body is almost completely see-through.

The copepod darts about with jerky motions.

Cyclops copepod

Females carry their eggs in pouches on either side of their body until they are ready to hatch.

DON'T MISS! Watch the cyclops as it escapes predators. It uses a sudden burst of energy to zoom away to safety.

IT'S WILD! The female uses a special chemical to help the male find her in open water so they can mate.

INDEX

A
acid 31, 37, 43
agriculture 9, 59, 68, 74, 155
allergies 102
amber 172
anatomy 10
antennae 10
    butterflies and moths 14, 15
    cockroaches 164
    ostracods 172
    true flies 106, 108
antifreeze chemicals 24, 168
antlions 141, 147
ants 6, 8, 9
    honeypot 45
    leafcutter 44
    pharaoh 9, 43, 46
    siafu 46
aphids 78
    black bean 123, 136
arachnids 82–103
arthropods 11
asexual reproduction 136, 153, 172
assassin bugs 124

B
bedbugs 123, 137
bees 8, 42–3, 54–5
    buff-tailed bumble 55
    hairy-legged mining 55
    honey 54–5, 103
    rusty-patched bumble 54, 55
    western honey 54, 55
beetles 10, 58–79
    American burying 60
    aquatic firefly 73
    bombardier 71
    Colorado 68
    darkling 67
    fire-colored 66
    flea 69
    giant stag 58, 63
    goliath 10, 72
    great diving 67
    harlequin 70
    Hercules 64–5
    jewel 68
    large copper dung 59, 62
    long-horned 59, 71
    pine chafer 69
    rove 61
    tortoise 70
    violin 61
    whirligig 66
bioluminescence 73
bloodsuckers 83, 98, 107, 109, 112, 114, 119, 137, 159–61
box-elder bugs 126
bugs
    as human food 155
    characteristics 10
    spotting 11
burrows 38, 55, 82, 86, 87, 94, 96, 157
butterflies 8, 10, 14–27
    American snout 16
    anise swallowtail 24, 25
    Apollo 23
    Baltimore checkerspot 22
    Cairns birdwing 23
    Canadian tiger swallowtail 24, 25
    Cleopatra 22
    giant swallowtail 25
    glasswing 16
    green hairstreak 27
    long-tailed skipper 27
    Monarch 8, 20–1
    orange oakleaf 14, 19
    orchard swallowtail 25
    painted lady 17
    paper kite 17
    peacock 10, 26
    pipevine swallowtail 24, 25
    postman 15, 19
    red cracker 18
    swallowtails 24–5
    tawny coster 18

C
caddisflies 141, 148
camouflage 14, 25, 59, 96, 97, 141, 146, 152, 153
cannibalism 99, 162
caterpillars 15, 25, 26, 29, 31, 36, 37, 39
cellulose 167
centipedes 141, 169
chrysalises 10, 21
cicadas, periodical 123, 130
climate change 9, 28
cockroaches, American 164
Coleoptera 58
colonies 42, 43, 44, 46, 47, 132, 165
color change 97
copepods, cyclops 173
courtship 110
crawlers 135
crickets
    field 157
    great green bush 157
    Jerusalem 156
crops 9, 11, 59, 68, 74, 155
crustaceans 170–3

D
damselflies 144
defense 123, 133, 154
demoiselles, banded 144
detritivores 59, 60, 62, 107, 108, 111
disease 98, 102, 114, 119, 124, 149
dobsonflies, eastern 145
dragonflies 141, 142–3
drumming 94, 150, 156

E
earwigs 154
echolocation 28
eggs 10, 43, 52, 90, 93, 115, 131, 134, 135, 159, 160, 171, 173
elytra 59, 63, 65
endangered species 9, 11, 21, 28, 74, 95, 100
exoskeletons 58, 59, 83, 93, 166
extinctions 9, 11
eyes
    arachnids 83
    compound 106, 112, 113
    small orders 142, 143, 146
    spiders 87, 88, 97
    true flies 106, 108, 112, 113

F
fairy flies 10, 51
false eyes 15, 39
famines 11
fangs, spiders 86, 97
fights 31, 60, 63, 64, 72, 74, 145
fireflies 73
fleas
    cat 161
    human 160
    water 171
flies 10
    black soldier 107, 111
    crane 10, 109
    deer 112
    drosophila fruit 110
    green bottle 116
    hairy bee 119
    horse 112
    house 113
    hover 107, 113
    robber 106, 118
    sand 109

stalk-eyed 108
tephritid fruit 110
tsetse 119
foam 131
fossils 99, 108, 161
froghoppers, meadow 131

G
galls 43, 53
grasshoppers, field 154

H
habitat loss 9
Haller's organ 98
halteres 107, 118
harvestmen 101
head lice 159
hibernation 37, 76, 116, 146
hickory horned devil 38
honeycomb 55
honeydew 133
hornets, Asian giant 9, 47
horns
    beetles 64
    true bugs 132, 134
Hymenoptera 42

I
insectivores 107, 122
insects 10

K
katydids, broad-winged 158
kings, termite 165

L
lacewings 141, 146
ladybugs 59, 76–9
    convergent lady beetle 77
    five-spot 78, 79
    orange 76
    seven-spot 9, 78
    ten-spot 78, 79

lantern bugs 134
larvae
    beetles 60, 62, 72, 73, 75, 76
    butterflies and moths 10, 15
    mosquitos 115
    needle midges 117
    small orders 141, 145, 147, 148, 161
    ticks 98
    true flies 107, 110, 111
    wasps 43, 53
leafhoppers 130
legs
    arachnids 82, 83
    butterflies 14
    small orders 140, 141, 169
Lepidoptera 14
life cycles
    butterflies 10
    dragonflies 143
    huntsman spiders 93
    ladybugs 76
    mosquitos 115
lifespans
    regal moths 38
    small orders 145, 148
    true flies 107
liquid feeders 107
locusts 11, 155

M
mantises 162–3
    devil's flower 162, 163
    European 162
    orchid 162, 163
    Texas unicorn 162, 163
mayflies 141, 149
meat-eaters 42
metamorphosis 10, 123, 141, 152
midges 116
    needle 117

migrations 18, 20
milkweed bugs 126
millipedes 141, 169
mimicry 59, 107, 140, 162
minstrel bugs 123, 127
mites 82, 102–3
    oribatid 102, 103
    red velvet 10
    varroa 102, 103
molting 10, 76, 83, 93, 137
mosquitos 114–15
    anopheles 115
    culex 114, 115
    tiger 107, 114, 115
moths 14–5, 28–39
    broad-bordered bee hawk 32
    cinnabar 34
    eight-spotted forester 35
    garden tiger 37
    giant leopard 33
    hawk 32
    Hercules 30
    Indian moon 29
    lobster 31
    luna 28, 29
    Madagascan sunset 30
    moon 28–9
    oleander hawk 32
    peppered 34
    Polyphemus 15, 36
    puss 39
    regal 38
    rosy maple 35
    Spanish moon 28, 29
    vampire 33
mounds, termite 165
mouthparts
    ants, wasps, and bees 43
    arachnids 82
    beetles 58, 63, 65
    small orders 156
    true bugs 123

N
naiads 143
nectar 55
nests 42, 44, 45, 47, 48, 49, 55, 74
nymphs 122, 123, 130, 131, 135, 136, 137, 143

O
ostracods 172
ovipositors 43, 52, 117, 157

P
parachutes 92
parasites 50–1, 53, 93, 98, 102–3, 107, 137, 141, 159–61
pedipalps 82
pesticides 9, 28, 54
pincers 83, 99, 100, 154
plant-eaters 42, 107, 122
planthoppers 134
poisonous bugs 15, 19, 34, 37, 73
pollination 9, 43, 54, 149
pollution 9, 144
proboscis 119, 161
pronotum 133
pseudoscorpions 100
pupae
    butterflies 10
    caddisflies 148
    ladybirds 76
    mosquitos 115
    wasps 43

Q
queens, termite 165

R
rostrums 151

S
saliva 107, 118, 131, 165
salt 14
sap-suckers 131, 132, 133, 135, 136
sawflies 52
scale insects 135
scavengers 107, 151
scorpionflies 140, 151
scorpions 82–3
　deathstalker 83, 99
shelters, caddisfly 148
shield bugs 127
shrimps, caridean 170
silk 26, 29, 85, 86, 89, 92, 93, 94
silverfish 167
sleeping sickness 119
slime 130
small orders 140–73
smells, defensive 125, 127, 146, 153, 156
soil 103, 111, 166
sounds
　beetles 65, 69, 71
　butterflies and moths 26
　small orders 150, 154, 156, 157, 158
　true bugs 122, 123, 125, 129, 130
spiderlings 92, 93
spiders 8, 82–97
　Brazilian wandering 94
　brown widow 90, 91
　curved spiny 84, 85
　dancing white lady 83, 94
　David Bowie huntsman 93
　European garden 84, 85
　flower crab 97
　funnel web 8, 86
　golden orb 84, 85
　heather 96
　house 92
　jumping 88, 92
　long-jawed orb weaver 85
　marbled orb weaver 85
　mouse 96
　northern black widow 91
　orb weavers 84–5
　raft 95
　red widow 91
　redback 91
　signature 85
　southern black widow 90, 91
　spitting 89
　sun 101
　tarantula 87
　trapdoor 87
　violin 89
　widow 90–1
　wolf 92
spinnerets 86
springtails 141, 168
stick insects 141, 152
　spiny leaf 153
stings
　scorpions 83, 99
　wasps and bees 43
stoneflies 141, 150
swarms, locust 155

T
tanaids 170
telsons 99
termites 165
　damp-wood 165
　soil 165
　spinifex 165
territory 23, 110, 144
thorax 10, 43, 82
thrips 149
ticks 82
　sheep 83, 98
treehoppers
　Brazilian 133
　oak 122, 132
true bugs 122–37
true flies 106–19

V
venom 86, 87, 89, 90, 94, 97, 99, 100, 118, 124, 125, 169
vibrations 82, 93, 95, 122, 133

W
waists 43, 49, 52, 53, 142
warning colors 14, 15, 19, 22, 59, 71, 127
wasps 42–3, 47–53
　chalcid 50
　eulophid 50, 51
　European 47
　gall 43, 53
　mud-dauber 49
　nasonia jewel 42, 51
　oak gall 53
　parasitic 50–1, 53
　potter 48, 49
　red velvet ant 48, 49
　sabre 50, 51
　solitary 48–9
　spider 49
　thread-waisted sand 49
　torymid 51
water bugs 128–9
　giant 128, 129
water fleas 171
water scorpions 128, 129
water boatmen 129
water striders 129
wax 55
webs
　caterpillars 26
　spiders 82, 84, 85, 86
weevils 74–5
　giraffe 74, 75
　New Guinea 75
　plantain 75
wheel bugs 124
wing cases, beetles 59, 63, 65, 67, 69, 72, 76, 77, 79
wings 10
　ants, wasps, and bees 43
　butterflies and moths 14, 15, 20
　small orders 140, 141
　true flies 106, 107
woodlice 9, 166
woolly bears 37
workers, termites 165

Z
zooplankton 173